Contents

Not God Enough, Lesson #1
Chapter #1: I Can't Believe! 1

Not God Enough, Lesson #2
Chapter #2: Your God Is Too Small
Chapter #3: He Is Not Silent 18

Not God Enough, Lesson #3
Chapter #4: Incomprehensible Wisdom
Chapter #5: Untouchable Holiness 37

Not God Enough, Lesson #4
Chapter #6: One Choice
Chapter #7: You Don't Get Your Own Personal Jesus . . 55

Not God Enough, Lesson #5
Chapter #8: The God We Crave. 74

Not God Enough, Lesson #6
Chapter #9: The God We Hate
Chapter 10: Scandalous 91

Not God Enough, Lesson #7
Chapter #11: How to Confuse an Angel
Chapter #12: Catching Fire 106

Not God Enough, Lesson #8
Chapter #13: It Is Not About You. 122

Not God Enough, Lesson #9
Chapter #14: He Wasn't Late After All
Chapter #15: Burning Hearts, Flaming Tongues 140

Not God Enough, Lesson #10
Chapter #16: Heaven At Your Back
Chapter #17: Bold Faith in a Big God 153

Not God Enough, Lesson #1
Chapter #1: I Can't Believe!
Good Questions Have Groups Talking
www.joshhunt.com

You might challenge your group to read the chapter(s) that go along with each week's study. I won't ask each week, but you might begin each session asking what everyone got out of this week's reading. Encourage them to read and mark their book and be ready to share.

OPEN:

What is one thing that is on your mind these days?

DIG

1. **Greear starts this book with the line, "For much of my life, I have struggled with faith." Can you relate? Have you struggled with faith?**

   I will tell you my secret: I have doubts.

   I have spent my life studying and thinking and reading and teaching about God. I grew up in the church. I went to a faith-based college and then to a seminary. I walked the straight and narrow. I never sowed any wild oats.

   And I have doubts.

I'll tell you more than that. There is a part of me that, after I die, if it all turns out to be true — the angels are singing, death is defeated, the roll is called up yonder and there I am — there is a part of me that will be surprised. What do you know? It's all true after all. I had my doubts.

Is it okay if we ask questions and consider objections and wonder out loud?

Is it okay if we don't pretend that everybody is split up into two camps: those who doubt and those who don't?

Is it possible — maybe even rational — to have faith in the presence of doubt?

Because I have faith too. And I have bet the farm. — John Ortberg, *Know Doubt: Embracing Uncertainty in Your Faith* (Grand Rapids, MI: Zondervan, 2014).

2. **I'd like to give you one more quote from Greear to chat about: "I've come to see that the problem—my lack of faith, my passionless heart, and my struggle to surrender—came from a fundamental deficiency in my vision of God." How does a deficiency in our vision of God affect us?**

What comes into our minds when we think about God is the most important thing about us.

The history of mankind will probably show that no people has ever risen above its religion, and man's spiritual history will positively demonstrate that no religion has ever been greater than its idea of God. Worship is pure or base as the worshiper entertains high or low thoughts of God.

For this reason the gravest question before the Church is always God Himself, and the most portentous fact about any man is not what he at a given time may say or do, but what he in his deep heart conceives God to be like. We tend by a secret law of the soul to move toward our mental image of God. This is true not only of the individual Christian, but of the company of Christians that composes the Church. Always the most revealing thing about the Church is her idea of God, just as her most significant message is what she says about Him or leaves unsaid, for her silence is often more eloquent than her speech. She can never escape the self-disclosure of her witness concerning God. — Tozer, *The Knowledge of the Holy*

3. **Last quote from Greear, then we will look at what the Bible says. This one is a little longer:**

> I am, in part, the product of a Christian culture that has fostered and promoted a small, domesticated view of God. The Western Christianity in which I have been immersed focuses on the practicality of faith. We present God as the best way to a happy and prosperous life. We show how God is the best explanation for unanswered questions and the best means to the life we desire. Our worship services seem more like pep rallies accompanied by practical tips for living than encounters with the living God who stands beyond time and whose presence is indescribably glorious. These shallow glimpses of God are fine as long as our faith remains untested, but they are utterly insufficient in the midst of serious questioning or intense suffering.

Ironically, our "diminished" God feels, for a while, easier to believe in. He acts in ways we can understand, explain, predict, and even control. He rarely offends us, so we are not embarrassed to talk about him with our friends. He helps us find our meaning and purpose. We think everyone should give him a try.

But in the end such a God cannot sustain faith.

Why can't a small view of God sustain faith?

We've been learning to face our fears. Pam Farrel challenges us to take the next steps—to trust God and embrace His adventure, move through life with boldness and daring, and achieve the dreams He's given us. "Show me the size of your God and I will show you the size of your confidence," Farrel often says. "Big God, big confidence. Big God, big courage. Big God, big-on bravery!" — Christin Ditchfield, What Women Should Know about Facing Fear: Finding Freedom from Anxious Thoughts, Nagging Worries, and Crippling Fears (Abilene, TX: Leafwood Publishers, 2013).

4. Matthew 28.17. After all they had seen, how in the world could they doubt?

The prevalence of doubt in the lives of God's children seems strange. Doubt is the antipole of the life of faith, yet it is common among believers. In fact, faith and doubt coexist in their experience (Matt. 14:3; 28:17; Luke 12:28–29). Because of "the remains of sin," doubt is a fact of life, differing from Christian to Christian only in frequency, degree, or length of experience.

Most of the passages in the New Testament where the word doubt occurs refer to the believer. This underscores the need to deal with doubt when it arises. It may come in times of financial difficulty, change of situation, bodily affliction, loss of a loved one, temptation, or persecution. In such times God's faithfulness to keep his promises (1 Kings 8:15, 56; 1 Cor. 10:13) may be forgotten, or dismissed. God has promised to the faithful: (1) the necessities of life without anxiety (Matt. 6:25–34); (2) good things of life with persecutions (Mark 10:28–30), and (3) conquest in all difficulties (Rom. 8:35–39). — R.C. Sproul, *Doubt & Assurance, electronic ed.* (Grand Rapids: Baker Book House, 2000).

5. **Before we get any further… What exactly does the word "doubt" mean? How is it different from unbelief?**

A recent Daily Telegraph poll put the use of the word 'literally' at the top of their most hated words or phrases, whereas another poll put 'at the end of the day' and 'fairly unique' at the top. One of my most hated phrases is 'with respect', a phrase that almost invariably will be followed by something not at all respectful. I think we often use the word 'doubt' in a similar way—'I very much doubt that' often means 'I am confident you are wrong', and 'I have my doubts' can mean 'I am about to tell you why you are wrong.' The word doubt, however, means nothing like this. It is the word that stands precisely between belief and unbelief; it is not weighted more to unbelief than to belief. It simply marks a lack of sureness. — Paula Gooder, *This Risen Existence: The Spirit of Easter* (Minneapolis, MN: Fortress Press, 2015), 33–34.

6. Is doubt sinful?

There is a difference between doubt and unbelief. Doubt is a matter of the mind: we cannot understand what God is doing or why He is doing it. Unbelief is a matter of the will: we refuse to believe God's Word and obey what He tells us to do. "Doubt is not always a sign that a man is wrong," said Oswald Chambers; "it may be a sign that he is thinking." In John's case, his inquiry was not born of willful unbelief, but of doubt nourished by physical and emotional strain.

You and I can look back at the ministry of Christ and understand what He was doing, but John did not have that advantage. John had announced judgment, but Jesus was doing deeds of love and mercy. John had promised that the kingdom was at hand, but there was no evidence of it so far. He had presented Jesus as "the Lamb of God" (John 1:29), so John must have understood something about Jesus' sacrifice; yet how did this sacrifice relate to the promised kingdom for Israel? He was perplexed about God's plan and his place in it. But let's not judge him harshly, for even the prophets were perplexed about some of these things (1 Peter 1:10–12). — Warren W. Wiersbe, *The Bible Exposition Commentary, vol. 1* (Wheaton, IL: Victor Books, 1996), 196–197.

7. Can you just decide to believe?

You cannot make yourself believe something through willpower. Oxford professor Richard Swinburne writes, "In general, a person cannot choose what to believe there and then. Belief is something that happens to a person, not something he or she does."

Sometimes people with "iffy" faith will think, I have to try harder to believe that I'm going to get the answer that I want to my prayer. It doesn't work. Trying hard to believe is toxic. It is a dangerous practice. I can say, "I'll try to learn. I'll try to study. I'll try to grow. I'll try to know God better. I'll try to pray." But I cannot directly generate belief through willpower.

Alice learned a lesson about the nature of beliefs on her trip to Wonderland. (Lewis Carroll was both an Oxford mathematician and an Anglican clergyman, so he was very interested in the nature of belief.) In the middle of a dizzying conversation, the Red Queen says to Alice, "Now I'll give you something to believe. I am 101 years, five months, and one day old."

This is too much for poor Alice. Although one would guess it is hard to gauge the age of an animated chess character, it is clear that the queen can't be beyond middle age.

"I can't believe that," said Alice.

"Can't you?" asked the queen, in a pitying tone. "Try again. Take a deep breath and shut your eyes."

Alice laughed. "There's no use trying," she said. "One can't believe impossible things."

"I daresay you haven't had much practice," said the queen. "When I was your age, I always did it for half an hour a day. Why, sometimes I believed as many as six impossible things before breakfast." — John Ortberg, *Know Doubt: Embracing Uncertainty in Your Faith* (Grand Rapids, MI: Zondervan, 2014).

8. **Here is a question we will return to a number of times in this study. I'd like to invite you to think**

about it during the week. What is the antidote to doubt?

An antidote for doubt is found in Jude 20–21. In the Greek text this is one sentence; its verb is the word keep (v. 21), which is surrounded by three participles. The sentence could be rearranged thus: "Begin right now, beloved, to keep yourselves in the love of God, by continually building yourselves up, by praying unceasingly, and by constantly looking for the mercy of our Lord Jesus Christ."

Edification, building upon the foundation of "your most holy faith" (see Jude 3), stands first. A precious stone in the foundation is God's love, demonstrated by the sacrifice of his Son for the sins of his people (John 3:14–17; Rom. 5:8; 1 John 4:10). The covenant blessing that flows therefrom is the forgiveness of all our iniquities (Matt. 26:28; Eph. 1:7; Heb. 8:12). The words "and [you will] hurl all our iniquities into the depths of the sea" (Mic. 7:19) are the basis of Andrew Bonar's reflection: "May we stand upon the shore of that ocean into which our sins have been cast, and see them sink to the depths, out of sight, and the sea calm and peaceful, the sunshine playing on it, the sunshine of Thy love and Thy favor."

Jude also urges effective prayer. To pray "in the Holy Spirit" (v. 20) brings life to the soul drowning in doubt. For this is prayer with divine assistance, articulation, fervor, favor (Rom. 8:26–27), assurance of God's love, and confidence in our adoption as God's very own (Rom. 5:5; 8:15).

Jude then demands the expectation of the "mercy of our Lord Jesus Christ to bring you to eternal life" (v. 21). This mercy he sends to us in this world (Pss. 23:6; 27:13–14;

Heb. 4:14–16) and the next (Pss. 23:6b; 73:24; John 17:24).

To those who occupy positions of leadership among his people, let us deal with doubt severely in our personal lives. Then let us exercise the patience and compassion of Christ toward those whom we are bound to help. "Be merciful to those who doubt" (Jude 22). — R.C. Sproul, *Doubt & Assurance, electronic ed.* (Grand Rapids: Baker Book House, 2000).

9. Proverbs 1.7. How does the fear of the Lord change us?

You'll never come to the point where you know enough about God. Knowing God is a lifelong pursuit that grows more rewarding as you learn more. It's not like studying physics or seventeenth-century British poets, where you get to the point of saying, "I've had enough!" Learning about God brings you peace (because you know He is in control), joy (because you know He wants the best for you), and a desire to know God better.

There is a danger in knowledge, however. You can substitute what you know about God objectively for actually knowing God personally. You aren't Sherlock Holmes, and God doesn't belong under a magnifying glass. He belongs in your heart, where He can change you into the person He wants you to be, reflecting His glory to others. — Bruce Bickel and Stan Jantz, *Keeping God in the Small Stuff* (Uhrichsville, OH: Barbour, 2013).

10. Why do you think knowledge starts with fearing God?

All truth therefore starts with what is true of God: who He is, what His mind knows, what His holiness entails, what His will approves, and so on. In other words, all truth is determined and properly explained by the being of God. Therefore, every notion of His nonexistence is by definition untrue. That is precisely what the Bible teaches: "The fool has said in his heart, 'There is no God' " (Psalm 14:1; 53:1).

The ramifications of all truth starting with God are profound. Returning to a point we touched on earlier: here is the reason why once someone denies God, logical consistency will ultimately force that person to deny all truth. A denial that God exists instantly removes the whole justification for any kind of knowledge. As Scripture says, "The fear of the LORD is the beginning of knowledge" (Proverbs 1:7).

So the necessary starting point for gaining authentic understanding of the fundamental concept of truth itself is an acknowledgment of the one true God. As Augustine said, we believe in order to understand, and our faith in turn is fed and strengthened as we gain better understanding. Both faith in God as He has revealed Himself and the understanding wrought by faith are therefore essential if we hope to apprehend truth in any serious and meaningful sense. — John F. MacArthur Jr., *The Truth War: Fighting for Certainty in an Age of Deception* (Nashville, TN: Thomas Nelson Publishers, 2007), xix.

11. Psalm 88.14 – 18. What is the writer feeling? Ever felt this way? Who has a story?

But what makes the psalm utterly grim is the closing line. Not only does Heman charge God with taking away his companions and loved ones, but in the last analysis, "the darkness is my closest friend" (88:18). Not God; the darkness.

One of the few attractive features of this psalm is its sheer honesty. It is never wise to be dishonest with God, of course; he knows exactly what we think anyway, and would rather hear our honest cries of hurt, outrage, and accusation than false cries of praise. Of course, better yet that we learn to understand, reflect, and sympathize with his own perspective. But in any case it is always the course of wisdom to be honest with God.

That brings up the most important element in this psalm. The cries and hurts penned here are not the cheap and thoughtless rage of people who use their darker moments to denounce God from afar, the smug critique of supercilious agnosticism or arrogant atheism. These cries actively engage with God, fully aware of the only real source of help. — D. A. Carson, *For the Love of God: A Daily Companion for Discovering the Riches of God's Word., vol. 1* (Wheaton, IL: Crossway Books, 1998), 25.

12. What advice would you have for the writer of this Psalm? What are we to do when we feel this way?

WHEN NOTHING SEEMS TO GO RIGHT, WHEN PEOPLE ARE NEGLECTING you and God seems to have forgotten you, don't stop praying. This troubled psalmist did not cease to pray. "LORD, I have called daily upon You; I have stretched out my hands to You" (v. 9). Even though the light is not shining, don't stop praying, because God will answer.

Start each day with the Lord. "But to You I have cried out, O LORD, and in the morning my prayer comes before You" (v. 13). Always begin your day with the Lord, and He will give you the strength to finish it.

Look to God alone. We have a tendency to trust circumstances, ourselves, and other people. Not the psalmist. He said, "I'm going to look to God alone. I'm going to trust the Lord of my salvation."

Yes, there are those dark, dismal, disappointing days. But God is still on the throne. Trust Him to see you through. — Warren W. Wiersbe, *Prayer, Praise & Promises: A Daily Walk through the Psalms* (Grand Rapids, MI: Baker Books, 2011), 226.

13. John 7.18ff. What is John feeling in this story?

C. S. Lewis experienced a crisis of faith after his wife died. He wrote that the danger he faced was not the danger of ceasing to believe in God, but the danger of starting to believe the wrong things about God. Lewis began to wonder if God was a cosmic sadist.

I understood exactly how he felt.

I began to see God as dangerous—a crusty old codger with total power to crush me at will. He could do whatever he wanted with me, and I was helpless to resist. — Daniel Hochhalter, *Losers like Us: Redefining Discipleship after Epic Failure* (Colorado Springs, CO: David C. Cook, 2014).

14. What is John's life situation? How might that have contributed to his doubt?

John had been in prison some months (Luke 3:19–20), but he knew what Jesus was doing because his own disciples kept him informed. It must have been difficult for this man, accustomed to a wilderness life, to be confined in a prison. The physical and emotional strain were no doubt great, and the long days of waiting did not make it easier. The Jewish leaders did nothing to intercede for John, and it seemed that even Jesus was doing nothing for him. If He came to set the prisoners free (Luke 4:18), then John the Baptist was a candidate!

It is not unusual for great spiritual leaders to have their days of doubt and uncertainty. Moses was ready to quit on one occasion (Num. 11:10–15), and so were Elijah (1 Kings 19) and Jeremiah (Jer. 20:7–9, 14–18); and even Paul knew the meaning of despair (2 Cor. 1:8–9). — Warren W. Wiersbe, *The Bible Exposition Commentary, vol. 1* (Wheaton, IL: Victor Books, 1996), 196.

15. 2 Corinthians 3.18. This verse varies quite a bit in the various translations, so let's look in up in several.

And we all, who with unveiled faces contemplate the Lord's glory, are being transformed into his image with ever-increasing glory, which comes from the Lord, who is the Spirit. 2 Corinthians 3:18 (NIV2011)

And we, who with unveiled faces all reflect the Lord's glory, are being transformed into his likeness with ever-increasing glory, which comes from the Lord, who is the Spirit. 2 Corinthians 3:18 (NIV)

And we all, with unveiled face, beholding the glory of the Lord, are being transformed into the same image from one degree of glory to another. For this comes from the Lord who is the Spirit. 2 Corinthians 3:18 (ESV)

But we Christians have no veil over our faces; we can be mirrors that brightly reflect the glory of the Lord. And as the Spirit of the Lord works within us, we become more and more like him. 2 Corinthians 3:18 (TLB)

All of us! Nothing between us and God, our faces shining with the brightness of his face. And so we are transfigured much like the Messiah, our lives gradually becoming brighter and more beautiful as God enters our lives and we become like him. 2 Corinthians 3:18 (MSG)

So our faces are not covered. They show the bright glory of the Lord, as the Lord's Spirit makes us more and more like our glorious Lord. 2 Corinthians 3:18 (CEV)

And all of us, with unveiled faces, seeing the glory of the Lord as though reflected in a mirror, are being transformed into the same image from one degree of glory to another; for this comes from the Lord, the Spirit. 2 Corinthians 3:18 (NRSV)

So all of us who have had that veil removed can see and reflect the glory of the Lord. And the Lord—who is the Spirit—makes us more and more like him as we are changed into his glorious image. 2 Corinthians 3:18 (NLT2)

We all, with unveiled faces, are looking as in a mirror at the glory of the Lord and are being transformed into the same image from glory to glory; this is from the Lord who is the Spirit. 2 Corinthians 3:18 (HCSB)

16. What do we learn about spiritual growth from this verse?

I love the Bible! It's richness and depth is amazing. You can squeeze the same passage every day and it will still bring more fresh insights. 2 Corinthians 3:18 is no exception. Let's look at this from the 1984 NIV:

And we, who with unveiled faces all reflect the Lord's glory, are being transformed into his likeness with ever-increasing glory, which comes from the Lord, who is the Spirit. 2 Corinthians 3:18 (NIV84)

Notice that instead of "beholding," the NIV84 has, "reflect." In the 2011 version, they changed it to, "contemplate." Let's look at it in a couple of other translations:

- Nothing between us and God, our faces shining with the brightness of His face. (MSG)

- We can be mirrors that brightly reflect the glory of the Lord. (TLB)

- So our faces are not covered. They show the bright glory of the Lord. (CEV)

- As all of us reflect the Lord's glory with faces that are not covered with veils… (GW)

The New Living has both meanings, "So all of us who have had that veil removed can see and reflect the glory of the Lord." 2 Corinthians 3:18 (NLT) So, is it behold, or reflect? Are we to look at Christ and be changed, or show Christ to others and be changed? I looked it up in a Greek dictionary for some help:

Κατοπτρίζομαι: behold; reflect

The word can mean behold or reflect. Here is the amazing thing: it makes good sense either way. We are changed as we behold Christ. We are changed as we reflect Christ to others.

As we tell others about Jesus, we become more like Jesus. As we boast to others about Jesus, Jesus changes us. As we talk about how great Jesus us, we are transformed into His image. — Johnny Hunt, *Changed* (Pulpit Press, 2014).

17. How does beholding Christ change us?

We become what we behold. We wind up like what we worship. We advance toward what we adore.

It is true in many arenas in life. Again, an example from tennis. Research shows that people who watch great tennis players become better. This is especially true if they imagine themselves moving like the pros.

> Many amateurs report that seeing tennis played at the highest level improves their own games.

> Watching tennis and playing it can be mutually helpful activities, dialectically entwined.

> Jon Levey, a writer and avid player said: "I always play better after watching the pros. Their form shows you that less is more. They move their body weight into the ball much better than I do. Everything seems to work in symmetry. After the Open, I suddenly know how to hit 'up' on my serve, like they do.

This is part of what makes idolatry so dangerous. Not only is it a slap in God's face, it is damaging to us. Idolatry hurts the idolater.

> What people revere, they resemble, either for ruin or restoration.

> God has made humans to reflect him, but if they do not commit themselves to him, they will not reflect him but something else in creation. At the core of our beings we are imaging creatures. It is not possible to be neutral on this issue: we either reflect the Creator or something in creation. — Josh Hunt, *How to Live the Christian Life*, 2016.

18. What is the difference between being transformed and trying really hard to be a good Christian?

Because there is none righteous, because none seeks after God (Romans 3:11), we are able to see the Lord only by His grace. Because He's lifted the veil from our eyes, we can look into His face. And in so doing, we are changed. We are changed not by a program, a practice, or a procedure. We are changed by a Person. We are changed by looking at Jesus—by spending time with Him, learning about Him, and worshiping Him.

Stay in the Scriptures, gang. Spend time in the Word daily. Come together for Bible study. Sing songs of adoration—for it's in worshiping, in studying, in looking at Him that you'll become like Him. — Jon Courson, *Jon Courson's Application Commentary* (Nashville, TN: Thomas Nelson, 2003), 1113.

19. What do you hope to learn from this study?

20. How can we pray for one another this week?

Not God Enough, Lesson #2
Chapter #2: Your God Is Too Small
Chapter #3: He Is Not Silent
Good Questions Have Groups Talking
www.joshhunt.com

You might challenge your group to read the chapter(s) that go along with each week's study. I won't ask each week, but you might begin each session asking what everyone got out of this week's reading. Encourage them to read and mark their book and be ready to share.

OPEN:

What was your greatest ambition as a kid?

DIG

1. **Psalm 19.1ff. How do the heavens declare the greatness of God? What exactly does that mean?**

   There is an old proverb that says, "If you would be alone, look at the stars."

   It was Emerson who commented that if the stars should come out only one night in a thousand years, everyone would drop what he or she was doing and in awe "look at the shining city of God." But because we see them all the time and because we are busy, we pay very little attention to the stars. We have too much noise and too many distractions! — A. W. Tozer and Ron Eggert, *The Tozer Topical Reader, vol. 2* (Camp Hill, PA: WingSpread, 1998), 41.

2. **When was the last time you looked—really looked—at the stars? What does it do to you to gaze at the heavens?**

First of all, the glory of God. Look in verse 1: "The heavens declare the glory of God" (Psalm 19:1). Go out some night, some starry night, and just look upward at that candelabra in the sky and think about all of that. Think of the glory that is displayed there.

Some time ago, Joyce and I took a vacation down to a little island in the Caribbean, a small little island. There were no automobiles on the island. And, we stayed in a little cabin that had no air conditioning, and right there by the water's edge. And, there was a wooden dock, a wharf—nothing to do. We made a big jigsaw puzzle— took us all week to do that. We walked the beach, and in order to go down to the little village there was a little boat out there. You had to take the little boat. And, the boat came with the cottage. But, for recreation, Joyce and I would go out and lie down on our backs on that little wharf, that little dock, at nighttime, and talk to one another, and look straight up into the stars—and down in the Caribbean, the sky, like the water, crystal clear. And, to see those stars up there, millions and millions of them, just to lie on your back and look at those stars, would just fill you with awe.

You know, we've forgotten to look up, haven't we? We're so busy running around. Some night, find a clear night and just go out and look up there and see what God has made. "The heavens declare the glory of God," amen?

You're going to see God's glory. — Adrian Rogers, "How You Can Know God Personally," in *Adrian Rogers Sermon Archive* (Signal Hill, CA: Rogers Family Trust, 2017), Ps 19.

3. Isaiah 40.26. What do we learn about God from this verse?

Isaiah 40, one of the Bible's greatest chapters, is addressed to homeless exiles in Babylonian refugee camps, people devastated by national and personal calamity. The message is simple: "Say to the cities of Judah, 'Here is your God!'" (v. 9).

Your God measures the waters in the hollow of His hand (v. 12). If you make a little cup with your palm and think of the vast, rolling oceans that cover most of Earth's surface, they're no more than a spoonful of water in the hollow of God's hand.

He has marked off the heavens with the span (v. 12), which is the distance between your thumb and fifth finger. The universe with its vast uncharted reaches fits nicely, as it were, in the span of God's omnipotent hand.

The nations are a drop in a bucket to Him (v. 15). The next time you water your plants, turn the bucket upside down and shake out the last drops. They're equivalent to America, Russia, China, India, and all the nations of the world in God's sight.

And the stars! "Look up and see: who created these? He brings out the starry host by number; He calls them all by name" (v. 26).

The conclusion: "Do you not know? Have you not heard? Yahweh is the everlasting God, the Creator of the whole earth. He never grows faint or weary; there is no limit to His understanding. He gives strength to the weary (vv.

28–29). — Robert J. Morgan, *All to Jesus* (Nashville: B&H, 2012).

4. Exodus 3. Look over this story silently. Who can summarize this story? Refresh our memories.

In Exodus 3, we read how God announced his name to Moses as "I AM WHO I AM" (v. 14)—a phrase of which "Yahweh" (Jehovah, "the LORD") is in effect a shortened form (v. 15). This name is not a description of God, but simply a declaration of his self-existence and his eternal changelessness; a reminder to mankind that he has life in himself, and that what he is now, he is eternally. In Exodus 34, however, we read how God "proclaimed his name, the LORD" to Moses by listing the various facets of his holy character. — J.I. Packer, *Knowing God*, 1973.

5. What does God reveal about Himself in this story?

Imagine you are Moses on that bizarre day long ago. You're out tending to your father-in-law's sheep, minding your own business, when suddenly, you see a bush on fire. You go in for a closer look, and the voice from the bush identifies itself as the voice of God. Then God tells you to take off your sandals.

If God appeared to us in a burning bush, we would naturally show respect to him. But we are also to respect God when he doesn't show up in miraculous ways. In the course of our daily lives, we need to remember that we are still dealing with the same God who can speak from a burning bush. We should still show God the same awe, respect, humility and obedience that Moses showed God that day.

God is more than worthy of our respect. Considering his almighty power and the fact that he's the one who made us, respecting him is really the least we can do.

— Christopher D. Hudson, *Niv, Once-a-Day: At the Table Family Devotional, Ebook* (Grand Rapids, MI: Zondervan, 2012).

6. **Someone might be thinking, "If I saw a burning bush, I would certainly have a big view of God. But, God doesn't show Himself to me that way, and my faith is flickering." What would you say to such a person?**

A minister had gradually lost his faith. In a world of great suffering, he could no longer feel the presence of the Lord in his own life. He was embittered that he had spent so much of his life in studying and pursuing an understanding of God. Now he had only a sense of betrayal and emptiness. Even his prayers seemed to bounce off an invisible barrier.

He expressed his anguish to an old friend he had known since his childhood. He told his friend that he thought he knew what Moses would have felt like if the burning bush had suddenly stopped burning and went up in a pale, gritty puff of smoke. He said that for him there was no more burning bush or sense of the presence of God in his life.

His friend, a rancher, confided that he, too, often felt that way. "But you know, Jack, I realized a while back that the burning bush is always there, always burning. It's just that I hadn't been spending much time in that part of the pasture."

Prayer is "that part of the pasture" where the bush is burning. If we are to be powerful in prayer, we must spend time there. — Billy Graham, *Hope for the Troubled Heart: Finding God in the Midst of Pain* (Nashville: Thomas Nelson, 2011).

7. Exodus 3.13 – 14. I am who I am. What does this mean? What does God reveal about Himself?

At the burning bush, God told Moses His name and said, "I AM WHO I AM" (Ex. 3:14). This signifies that the central characteristic of the God of the Bible is existence. His very nature is existence. Popeye can say, "I am what I am." But only God can say, "I AM WHO I AM." He is the "I AM." The Bible also calls God eternal (Col. 1:17; Heb. 1:2), unchanging (Mal. 3:6; Heb. 6:18), infinite (1 Kings 8:27; Isa. 66:1), all-good (Ps. 86:5; Luke 18:19), and all-powerful (Heb. 1:3; Matt. 19:26). Since these beings are the same in all these respects, and there can't be two infinite beings, then this God that the arguments point us to is the God of the Bible. — Norman L. Geisler and Ronald M. Brooks, *When Skeptics Ask* (Wheaton, IL: Victor Books, 1990), 29.

8. Exodus 34. This is the story of the giving of the 10 Commandments, Take II. Look over the story silently. What does God reveal about Himself in this story?

Moses wanted to know something more of God, so he pleaded with Him, "Please, show me Your glory" (Exodus 33:18).

God responded by taking Moses aside and putting him in the cleft of a rock. Then He revealed Himself to Moses in all His glory (see 34:6–7). The way God wants us to know His glory is through the revelation of His great love toward humankind. That is just what He revealed to Moses.

Often when we think about the glory of God, we think of His majesty and splendor, His power and dominion. This is not the glory He wants us to know Him by. The Lord is forever waiting to show us His love—to forgive us, show us mercy and restore us to Himself.

Up to this point, Moses had viewed the Lord as a God of law and wrath. Moses had trembled with terror in the Lord's presence as he pled with Him on behalf of Israel. Now, however, at the first sight of God's glory, Moses was no longer fearful of the Lord. Instead, he was moved to worship because he saw God's nature of love, kindness and mercy.

Once we receive a revelation of God's glory, our worship cannot help but change. Each new revelation of His love brings supernatural change. — David Wilkerson, *God Is Faithful: A Daily Invitation into the Father Heart of God* (Grand Rapids, MI: Chosen, 2012).

9. **The title of this chapter is: Your God Is Too Small. What problems does a small view of God cause?**

I am positively sure after many years of observation and prayer that the basis of all of our trouble today, in religious circles, is that our God is too small.

When he says magnify the Lord, he doesn't mean that you are to make God big, but you are to see Him big. When we take a telescope and look at a star, we don't make the star bigger, we only see it big. Likewise you cannot make God bigger, but you are only to see Him bigger....

What is the most important verse in the Bible? It is not the one you think it is: "Jesus Christ the same yesterday, and to day, and for ever" (Hebrews 13:8). Nor is it the other one you think it is: John 3:16, "For God so loved the world...."The most important verse in the Bible is this one: "In the beginning God..." (Genesis 1:1). That is the most important verse, because that is where everything must begin. God is the mountain out of which everything springs, and He is the foundation upon which everything rests. God is all in all. — A. W. Tozer and Ron Eggert, *Tozer on the Almighty God: A 365-Day Devotional* (Chicago, IL: Moody Publishers, 2015).

Chapter #3: He Is Not Silent

10. John 1.14 – 18. What do we learn about God from this passage?

God is a communicating God. He is the Word (John 1:1), and, in the form of Jesus Christ, "the Word was made flesh, and dwelt among us" (John 1:14). The Word created all things (John 1:3), and by His command all things came to be (Ps. 148:5). Since God seeks to be known in those things that are made, it is not surprising that evidence of a communicating being should be seen throughout His creation. — Kurt P. Wise, *Faith, Form, and Time: What the Bible Teaches and Science Confirms about Creation and the Age of the Universe* (Nashville, TN: Broadman & Holman, 2002), 99–100.

11. Perhaps someone is thinking. "God speaks, sure. I have never heard Him speak." What would you say to such a person?

Throughout history God has spoken. For millennia, he has forged his children's faith by promising parted waters, empowering unlikely leaders, declaring world-changing prophecies—and imparting last-minute sermons to pastors who questioned whether he really would deliver. In short, our God is a communicating God. Always has been, and always will be. And if there is one story in Scripture that goes to great lengths to prove this point, it's the story of Elijah, the prophet described in 1 Kings as a man who was "zealous for God."

There comes a point in Elijah's remarkable ministry when his zealotry has fizzled to zero. He is ready to call it quits. "I've been working my heart out," he says to God, and for what? "The people of Israel have abandoned your covenant, destroyed the places of worship and murdered your prophets. I'm the only one left, and now they're trying to kill me."

Elijah felt undone, and perhaps the only thing that could improve his mood was a firsthand encounter with God.

As the story goes, Elijah trekked into the desert and eventually collapsed from exhaustion under the shade of a tree. It was here that an angel who happened to be in the area gave him specific instructions for where he could go to experience the presence of God. The instructions took Elijah forty days and forty nights to follow, but eventually he ended up at Horeb, the mountain that the angel had told him to find. He crawled his way into a cave and got some much-needed sleep.

The next day, the Lord said to Elijah, "Go, stand on the mountain at attention before God. God will pass by." Enter whisper number one. Elijah's weariness gave way to wonder. I imagine his heart beating a little faster as he considered what it would be like to meet firsthand the One he had served all these years.

Elijah obeyed the whisper and hiked up the mountain. The Bible describes a hurricane-force wind howling past Elijah as he stood on that mountain's face. Strength, might, power, brute force—"That's probably God," Elijah must have thought. Yet the text says, "But God wasn't to be found in the wind."

Next up came a full-fledged, mountain-trembling earthquake. But again, God was not there.

A fire then blazed by, consuming everything on the side of the mountain but Elijah himself—yet to his sure surprise, his God was not to be found in the flames.

Finally, the text says, following the fire came a "gentle and quiet whisper." And amazingly, that's where Elijah found God.

The wind, the earthquake, the fire—none of these conduits of God's company would have shocked Elijah as much as the still, small voice that emerged. In response, he "muffled his face with his great cloak, went to the mouth of the cave, and stood there."

"So Elijah, now tell me, what are you doing here?" God whispered. Elijah then told God all of his frustrations, unburdening himself from the emotional poundage he'd been carrying. I envision Elijah—enveloped by God's audible whisper, his shoulders relaxing with each syllable he spoke—thinking, "Am I glad you're here!" Nothing else can ease the soul like the presence of our Holy God.

On Mount Horeb that day, Creator convened with creation, and one man's life was forever changed. Regardless of what else Elijah might have later told his friends about this encounter—and about God himself—undoubtedly he had been a witness to two attributes at the very core of who God is: he's relational and he is near.

He is all-powerful, yes. He is righteous and holy too. He is sovereign, he is majestic, he is magnificent, he is just. But what stunned Elijah on the side of that mountain—and what will stun you someday if it hasn't already—is that the same God who is all-powerful, all-knowing, all-everything, yearns to be in relationship with us. The God of the Scriptures is irrepressibly communal, hopelessly familial, and his whispers are still ours to hear. — Bill

Hybels and Wayne Cordeiro, *The Power of a Whisper: Hearing God, Having the Guts to Respond* (Grand Rapids, MI: Zondervan, 2010).

12. 2 Corinthians 3.16 – 17. God sometimes speaks through a whisper. What is the main way He speaks?

Second Timothy 3:16 speaks of the inspiration of Scripture. "Inspired" is the translation of a Greek word that literally means "God-breathed." Every word of Scripture is from the mouth of God!

Theologians speak of inspiration as the mysterious process by which God worked through the authors of Scripture to produce inerrant and divinely authoritative writings. Inspiration is a mystery because Scripture doesn't explain specifically how it occurred. The only glimpse we have is from 2 Peter: "Know this first of all, that no prophecy of Scripture is a matter of one's own interpretation, for no prophecy was ever made by an act of human will, but men moved by the Holy Spirit spoke from God" (1:20–21).

"Interpretation" speaks of origin. Scripture didn't originate on the human level but with the Holy Spirit, who "moved" upon the authors to write it (v. 21). "Moved" is the translation of a nautical term that describes the effects of wind upon a ship as it blows against its sails and moves it through the water. Similarly, the Spirit moved on the Biblical writers to produce the Word of God in the language of men.

The human authors of Scripture knew they were writing God's Word, and they did so with confidence and authority. Often they cited or alluded to one another as authoritative agents of divine revelation (e.g., 2 Peter 3:15–16).

On a personal level, inspiration guarantees that what Scripture says, God says. It's His counsel to you; so you can study and obey it with full assurance that it is true and will never lead you astray. — John F. MacArthur Jr., *Drawing Near—Daily Readings for a Deeper Faith* (Wheaton, IL: Crossway Books, 1993), 299.

13. God speaks through a whisper. He speaks through His Word. How else does God speak?

Primary ways God speaks to us

1. God Speaks Through the Bible

"Every part of Scripture is God-breathed and useful in one way or another—showing us truth, exposing our rebellion, correcting our mistakes, training us to live God's way." 2 Timothy 3:16 (MSG)

2. God Speaks Through Impressions of the Holy Spirit

"The Holy Spirit … will teach you all things and will remind you of everything I have said to you." John 14:26 (NIV)

3. God Speaks Through People

"So faith comes from hearing, that is, hearing the Good News about Christ." Romans 10:17

4. God Speaks To Us Through Difficulties

"Before I was afflicted I went astray, but now I obey your word. You are good, and what you do is good; teach me your decrees." Psalm 119:67–68 (NIV)

5. God Speaks Through His Creation

"The heavens declare the glory of God ... day after day they pour forth speech; night after night they display knowledge." Psalm 19:1–2

6. God Speaks Through Circumstances

"And we know that God causes everything to work together for the good of those who love God and are called according to his purpose for them." Romans 8:28 (NLT)

7. God Speaks Through Angels

"Angels are only servants, spirits sent to care for people who inherit salvation." Hebrews 1:14 (NLT)

8. God Speaks to Us By Giving Us Blessings

"Every good and perfect gift is from above, coming down from the Father." James 1:17 (NIV)

Vern Heidebrecht, *Hearing God's Voice* (Colorado Springs, CO: David C Cook, 2010).

14. 2 Timothy 3.16, 17 says that scripture is useful for doctrine or teaching. Doctrine sounds like a bit of a stuffy word. Why does doctrine matter? Why is doctrine important?

Belief affects behavior. Doctrine matters. — Nancy DeMoss Wolgemuth, *Adorned: Living out the Beauty of the Gospel Together* (Chicago, IL: Moody Publishers, 2017).

15. All Scripture is useful for doctrine, or teaching. It is also useful for rebuke. Would you like it better if it didn't rebuke? Why is rebuke a good thing?

Paul also gives Timothy instructions about the tone of his preaching. He uses two words that carry negative connotations and one that is positive: reprove, rebuke, and exhort (2 Tim. 4:2). All valid ministry must have a balance of positive and negative. The preacher who fails to reprove and rebuke is not fulfilling his commission.

I recently listened to a radio interview with a preacher who assiduously avoids any mention of sin in his preaching because he feels people are burdened with too much guilt anyway. The interviewer asked how he could justify such a policy. The pastor replied that he had made the decision to focus on meeting people's needs, not attacking their sin.

But people's deepest need is to confess and overcome their sin. So preaching that fails to confront and correct sin through the Word of God does not meet people's need. It may make them feel good. And they may respond enthusiastically to the preacher, but that does not mean such preaching meets real needs.

To reprove, rebuke, and exhort is to preach the Word, for those are the very same ministries Scripture accomplishes: "All Scripture is inspired by God and profitable for teaching, for reproof, for correction, for training in righteousness" (2 Tim. 3:16). Notice the same balance of positive and negative tone. Reproof and correction are negative; teaching and training are positive. — John F. MacArthur Jr., *Ashamed of the Gospel: When the Church Becomes like the World* (Wheaton, IL: Crossway Books, 1993), 33–34.

16. Next, correction. What is the difference between rebuke and correction?

When I was in school, I appreciated those teachers who marked wrong answers on my papers and then wrote in the correct ones. But those who only marked wrong answers without indicating what was correct frustrated me. Scripture is not like those schoolteachers who would merely mark wrong answers. It actually corrects us. The Greek word for "correction" in 2 Timothy 3:16 literally means "to straighten up." God's Word doesn't just rebuke, convict, and refute. It goes further and pulls us back into line, mending, rebuilding, and fixing what is broken.

Not unlike the relationship parents have with their children, spiritual mothers and fathers reprove their children regarding sins and areas that need improvement. If they are good parents, they will then set their children on the correct path by teaching them appropriate behaviors and attitudes.

Scriptural correction therefore is the positive provision for believers who accept the Word's negative reproof. The process sometimes "for the moment seems not to be joyful, but sorrowful; yet to those who have been trained by it, afterwards it yields the peaceful fruit of righteousness" (Heb. 12:11). — John MacArthur, *The Pillars of Christian Character: The Basic Essentials of a Living Faith* (Wheaton, IL: Crossway Books, 1998), 77–78.

17. Training in righteousness. What exactly is that talking about?

If we're allowing God's Word to have an authentic role in our spiritual growth, it will not just leave us with the bare elements of truth. Instead, the Word will apply to our lives what it has taught us so that it might continually build us up in righteousness. In 2 Timothy 3:16 this process is denoted by the Greek word paideia, which is rendered "training" and originally meant training a child (paidion) but came to have a broader meaning of any sort of training, as it does in this verse.

But how does training in righteousness express itself practically? The process begins when we hear Scripture preached during the worship service or taught in a Sunday school class or Bible study. That's when we store doctrinal and biblical truth in our hearts and minds.

The next practical phase of our training in righteousness comes in our daily lives as we interact with people and ideas of the world and occasionally need to confront error. You might find yourself in a group discussion when someone interjects an obvious doctrinal error. At that point you can draw on Scripture to refute the error and allow the truth to shape the thinking of the other people in the group. In that way you will be obeying the apostle Paul's command to present yourselves "approved to God as a workman who does not need to be ashamed, handling accurately the word of truth" (2 Tim. 2:15; cf. Eph. 6:14–17).

On a more personal level you can be trained in righteousness when you encounter a temptation. When you think you may be on the verge of losing a battle with temptation, you can draw on your knowledge of Scripture to help you respond in a righteous and godly way. Similarly, you may face a major trial in which your understanding of the Word will take over, guide you through the crisis, and thereby further train you in righteousness. Following the example of the Lord Jesus (see Matt. 4:3–10), we need to carefully and accurately use Scripture to deal with each and every temptation or trial from the world (cf. Ps. 119:9–11; Col. 3:16).

No matter how deep our understanding of Scripture is, God still trains us in ways we don't always comprehend. However, that should not keep us from affirming with the psalmist, "As the deer pants for the water brooks, so my soul pants for Thee, O God" (Ps. 42:1). — John MacArthur, *The Pillars of Christian Character: The Basic Essentials of a Living Faith* (Wheaton, IL: Crossway Books, 1998), 78–79.

18. What is the difference between training and trying hard to be good?

Imagine you can't play the piano and I asked you to play Amazing Grace. Would it be easy or hard? Would it help if you tried really, really hard to play Amazing Grace?

This is how many people try to live the Christian life. They hear a sermon on gratefulness. They try really hard to be grateful. They do this for a few hours or a few days. Then, they forget about it. Life gets in the way. Then, they are left with a nagging feeling of guilt about how they are not as grateful as they would like to be.

Next week they hear a sermon on service. They try really hard to serve... for a few hours. Then they forget about it. Again, they have a life. They don't rebel against God or the idea of serving, they just forget about it and go on with life. But again, they are left with a nagging sense of guilt about not serving as they ought.

The next week they hear a sermon on prayer. Same thing.

There is a better way. (I owe my insight into this verse to John Ortberg. I think he got it from Dallas Willard.) Here is the key verse:

Train yourself to be godly. 1 Timothy 4:7 (NIV2011)

Let's go back to the piano. Instead of trying really hard to play Amazing Grace, what if you trained yourself to play Amazing Grace? What would that look like?

Let's imagine you sit down with a skilled piano teacher. He explains that your fingers can be numbered one through five. The thumb is one and the pinky is five. The middle finger is three.

He places your middle finger on the E above middle C. He asks you to play 3-2-1 starting with E above middle C with the middle finger of your right hand. These are the first three notes of "Mary had a little lamb." He walks you through the rest of the song, pointing to the notes on the music in front of you. After about ten times, you stumble through it.

He gives you ten more songs, and works you through each one until you are able to figure out how it works. He asks you to practice for an hour a day and you agree to do so. A week later, you can play the melody of all ten songs reasonably well. You are only playing one note at a time at this point.

He gives you ten more songs. You practice those for a few weeks. He introduces the left hand. At first, you play only the left hand. Then, you play both hands together. Then you play two notes at the same time in the right hand. This is called harmony. You practice some more. Practice, practice, practice. This is training to play the piano.

Keep this up for about five years and you will easily be able to play Amazing Grace. It won't be hard; it will be easy.

You might object that this way sounds like a hard way to learn to play Amazing Grace. It is not the hard way, it is the only way. The hard way is trying really hard to play Amazing Grace. Here is the good news. Once you subject yourself to this training, playing Amazing Grace will be easy. In fact, nearly any song in the hymnbook will be easy. Ask anyone who can play Amazing Grace. They will tell you it is easy. What is hard is trying to do something you have not trained yourself to do. — Josh Hunt, *How to Live the Christian Life*, 2016.

19. **What did you learn today? What do you want to remember?**

20. **How can we pray for one another today?**

Not God Enough, Lesson #3
Chapter #4: Incomprehensible Wisdom
Chapter #5: Untouchable Holiness
Good Questions Have Groups Talking
www.joshhunt.com

OPEN:

What was the most difficult year of your life so far?

DIG

1. **I can't prove it, but I have a hunch that the #1 cause of people losing their faith is tragedy. Stated in the form of a question: if God is all good, and all powerful, why would He let _____ happen. Or, as the Babylonian Bee has it, "If God Is Both All-Good And All-Powerful, Why Did He Allow The Star Wars Prequels?" ⏴ Have you seen people lose their faith because of a tragedy? Who has a story?**

    On the other hand, if you were to ask me why I doubt, I suppose I would tell you a story about a baby as well. A couple whom I have known for a long time had a beautiful little daughter. She was the kind of child who was so beautiful that people would stop them on the street to comment on her beauty. They were the kind of parents you would hope every child might have.

    They had a pool in their backyard.

One summer day it was so nice outside that the mom set up the playpen in the backyard so that her daughter could enjoy the day. The phone rang, and her daughter was in the playpen, so she went in to answer the phone. Her daughter tugged on the wall of that playpen, and the hinge that held the side up gave way. It didn't have to. God could have stopped it. God could have reached down from heaven and straightened it out and kept that playpen up. He didn't. The hinge gave way, and the side came down, and the baby crawled out, and heaven was silent.

When that mom came outside, she saw the beautiful little body of her beloved daughter at the bottom of that pool. It was the beginning of a pain that no words could name. She would have died if doing so could have changed that one moment. But she could not. She would have to live. The memory of how old her daughter would be would have to haunt her every birthday and every Christmas and on the day she would have graduated from high school. That mom would live with the emptiness, the guilt, the blame, and the aloneness.

When that little baby left this world, she left behind a world that was God-silent.

Dostoyevsky, who was a believer, wrote that the "death of a single infant calls into question the existence of God." — John Ortberg, *Know Doubt: Embracing Uncertainty in Your Faith* (Grand Rapids, MI: Zondervan, 2014).

2. Why is it important that we take this issue seriously and not be glib when people tell us their stories?

When people of faith are not willing to sit quietly sometimes and let doubt make its case, bad things can happen.

Sometimes people of faith can be glib. Sometimes they respond with bad answers.

Sometimes preachers add enormous pain by telling people they have brought suffering on themselves by sinning. Sometimes they tell people they have not been delivered because they do not have enough faith.

Sometimes people want to believe but find they can't.

I think of a man who prayed for his alcoholic father for twenty years — but his father never changed.

I think of a woman who prayed for a mentally ill sister who committed suicide.

I think of a brilliant young girl who was neglected by her mom, abandoned by her dad, and molested by her uncle. She was an atheist at age eleven and then through a group of friends became a Christian. But she was tormented with sexual addictions all through her teenage years. She began to be troubled by the thought that some people were condemned to hell just because they belonged to a different religion. She kept asking God to help her; she kept asking for answers, but nothing seemed to change.

I think of a letter I received recently:

> How can I believe a Jewish friend who is devoted to God and hears him better than I do will go to hell and I will go to heaven even though I'm not as good

as he is, just because I am a Christian and he is not? Will the real God and creator of the universe stand up?

The God I used to believe in was very easy to hear and follow. Now I'm in the dark, and he feels like a stranger. I'm praying but am getting nervous that he won't answer because I now have so little faith . . . not even the size of a grain of mustard seed.

Philosopher André Comte-Sponville writes poignantly about the beauty of humility: "Humility may be the most religious of virtues. How one longs to kneel down in churches!" But he said he could not bring himself to do this because he would have to believe that God created him, and human beings seem to him too wretched to permit that possibility. "To believe in God would be a sin of pride." — John Ortberg, *Know Doubt: Embracing Uncertainty in Your Faith* (Grand Rapids, MI: Zondervan, 2014).

3. What is the answer to this question: why does a good God let bad things happen?

God is still there despite any tragedy you may be experiencing. But why does God allow suffering?

On Nov. 21, 1980, when the MGM Grand Hotel in Las Vegas burned, survivors were brought into the Convention Center, where our Crusade meetings were being held. In an interview, Governor Robert List talked about the good times at the MGM only 24 hours before. "And how quickly," he said, "the music has stopped."

Some day, for all of you, if you don't know God, the music will stop. It will all be over. The Bible says, "It is appointed for men to die once, but after this the judgment" (Hebrews 9:27).

The Bible says that Job suddenly lost all of his wealth and his children. The devil said to God, "If You take all those possessions away from him, he'll curse You and turn from You." But God replied, "You can do anything to him, except you can't kill him, and then we'll see" (Cf. Job 1:11-12).

Job never asked why those things were happening to him. The closest he ever came was when he said, "Show me why You contend with me" (Job 10:2). Job was sharing his agony of spirit with the very God he could not understand.

Suffering carries a message of mystery. The Bible says, "Great is the mystery of godliness" (1 Timothy 3:16). When I was asked to explain the tragedy of the fire at the MGM Grand Hotel, I had to say, "There's a mystery to tragedies like this. We don't know the answer." And we may never know until God explains all things to us. — Billy Graham https://billygraham.org/story/suffering-why-does-god-allow-it/

4. **What do we need to remember when our time to suffer comes—and, it will come.**

Advice   for handling hardships is plentiful, found in whole books or simple   slogans such as, "When life hands you a lemon, make lemonade." As a   physician who regularly sees people endure multiple losses, I have   thought a lot about what to say to them. I know for certain that quips   about lemons and lemonade won't be enough to keep them from despairing   or feeling their disappointment in God. No, we should never give trite   responses to others, especially when they are experiencing great   difficulties. I do not believe we should teach difficult concepts (such   as those we will review later in this chapter) to those in the midst of much suffering, either. When someone is suffering, it is often best to offer our presence and our compassion, along with our tears.

The Bible offers many insights that help us to endure difficulties well—insights that are far from being trite. The key is that we must study and understand these truths before it is our turn to suffer. The church should be preparing the saints to suffer well. There is a Christian way to avoid being defeated by end of-life adversities, as distressing as they might be. I describe it in strategy 4: Grow through Adversity.

Though it may be a radical idea, the Bible tells us that instead of separating us from God, suffering has the potential to bring us nearer to him. I call that "suffering productively." — John Dunlop, *Finishing Well to the Glory of God: Strategies from a Christian Physician* (Wheaton, IL: Crossway, 2011).

5. Ecclesiastes 8.17. What do we learn about God from this verse?

God's work is wonderful, but at times incomprehensible. — John MacArthur Jr., ed., *The MacArthur Study Bible, electronic ed.* (Nashville, TN: Word Pub., 1997), 935.

6. God is incomprehensible. What is the application? How does it affect us?

When David pondered the imponderable mind of God, he saw all of that infinite intellect directed toward him, and it swelled his heart with joy! "How precious are your thoughts about me, O God!" he exclaimed. "They are innumerable! I can't even count them; they outnumber the grains of sand! And when I wake up in the morning, you are still with me!" (Ps. 139:17–18, NLT).

David saw the very same mind-boggling, mysterious God who had stunned Isaiah and humbled Job. But David's awe was golden with comfort—and boundless love. David knew that all of the greatness and mystery of God was for him. This God—whom he couldn't figure out and didn't really need to figure out—happened to love David and be on David's side!

The son of Jesse didn't pretend to understand that, nor did he worry much about it. He just believed it and gloried in it. He took it to the bank and drew on the account for the rest of his days.

Depending upon how you look at it, then, the greatness and mystery of God either flattens you like a bug on the windshield or brings inexpressible comfort and rest.

Rest? Can you rest in a mystery? Can you pillow your head on an incomprehensible God, as a child sleeps in a 747 thundering 40,000 feet over the midnight wastes of the Arctic? — *Discipleship Journal, Issue 102* (November/December 1997) (NavPress, 1997).

7. What do we learn about ourselves from this verse?

Since our observation is limited, we cannot figure everything out. One of the main reasons we cannot figure everything out in this cursed world is because things do not always work out the way they are supposed to work out (8:14-17). Living by wisdom does not always make life go smoothly. Why? What is going on? Why is there suffering? Why do these wisdom principles not work? The problem is that humanity has departed from God's design. The Bible calls this departure "sin," and sin leads to brokenness and meaninglessness. — Daniel L. Akin et al., Exalting Jesus in Ecclesiastes (Nashville, TN: Holman Reference, 2016).

8. Romans 8.18 – 22. What do we learn about suffering from this passage?

The apostle, always one to encourage, makes one of the most comforting statements in all of the Bible regarding our suffering with Christ. I like the NEB translation, "For I reckon that the sufferings we now endure bear no comparison with the splendor that is as yet unrevealed, which is in store for us."

John Murray notes that

> this verse is an appeal to the great disproportion between the sufferings endured in this life and the weight of glory reserved for the children of God—the present sufferings fade into insignificance when compared with the glory to be revealed in the future. The apostle appeals to this consideration an inducement to patient endurance of sufferings. — Edward F. Murphy, *Handbook for Spiritual Warfare* (Nashville: Thomas Nelson, 1996).

9. What do we learn about that time when all suffering will cease—what do we learn about Heaven?

So the sufferings of this present time are nothing more than light afflictions and they are to last but for a moment. And when this little moment is finished we shall leave moments forever, going out of time and into eternity. Well we may reckon that just as a moment may not be compared with eternity so our light afflictions, our sufferings of the present time, are not worthy to be compared with the glory that shall be revealed in us.

Nothing can be said about the future glory that could describe it on our present senses. Any and all descriptions of that glory must be understatements because of the insufficiency of our senses. How can the finite encompass the infinite? How can the eternal state be grasped by a creature in time? "It does not yet appear what we shall be" (1 John 3:2). Only the heart can know the language that will do justice to this: "We shall see Him as He is." What is worth comparing with that transforming sight? — Donald Grey Barnhouse, *God's Heirs: Romans 8:1–39* (Grand Rapids, MI: William B. Eerdmans Publishing Company, 1963), 125.

Chapter #5: Untouchable Holiness

10. Isaiah 6.1 – 5. What do we learn about God from this passage?

From his call vision, Isaiah derived his characteristic understanding of God as majestic, holy, and glorious. Isaiah saw the Lord majestically towering over him, seated on a lofty throne, so that the skirts of His robe filled the temple. The Lord was surrounded by the seraphim, angelic attendants whose name means "burning ones." Their cries of praise shook the doorposts of the temple, and smoke filled the building.

This God is also holy and not like human beings with their sinful compromises. Isaiah's favorite title for God is "the Holy One of Israel" (1:4; 5:19, 24; etc.). His ways are not like ours, nor are His thoughts (55:8, 9). For sinful Israel to find themselves in the hands of such a holy God is not good news.

He is also the glorious God, before whom the nations are as a drop in a bucket and their idols even less significant (40:15). He created all things and rules over all (45:5–12). In the end, all nations will come to acknowledge this truth and bow down before the one true God, so that the earth will be as filled with His glory as the divine throne room in heaven (6:3; 40:5; 66:18). — R. C. Sproul, ed., *The Reformation Study Bible: English Standard Version (2015 Edition)* (Orlando, FL: Reformation Trust, 2015), 1116.

11. What do we know about Isaiah? You might scan over the introduction in your Study Bible.

The prophet in Old Testament Israel was a lonely man. He was a rugged individualist singled out by God for a painful task. He served as a prosecuting attorney of sorts, the appointed spokesman of the Supreme Judge of heaven and earth to bring suit against those who had sinned against the bench.

The prophet was not an earthly philosopher who wrote his opinions for scholars to discuss; he was not a playwright who composed dramas for public entertainment. He was a messenger, a herald of a cosmic king. His announcements were prefaced by the words "Thus saith the Lord."

The record of the lives of the prophets reads like a history of martyrs. Their history sounds like a casualty report from the Third Division in World War II. The life expectancy of a prophet was that of a marine lieutenant in combat.

When it is said of Jesus that He was despised and rejected of men, a man of sorrows and acquainted with grief, it is clear that He stood in a long line of men whom God had appointed to such suffering. The prophet's curse was solitude; his home was often a cave. The desert was his traditional meeting place with God. Nakedness was sometimes his wardrobe, a wooden stock his necktie. His songs were composed with tears.

Such a man was Isaiah Ben Amoz.

In the panoply of Old Testament heroes, Isaiah stands out in stellar relief. He was a prophet of prophets, a leader of leaders. He is called a "major prophet" because of the vast size of the written material that bears his name.

As a prophet, Isaiah was unusual. Most prophets were of humble origins: peasants, shepherds, farmers. Isaiah was of the nobility. He was a recognized statesman, having access to the royal court of his day. He consorted with princes and kings. God used him to speak to several monarchs of Judah, including Uzziah, Jotham, Ahaz, and Hezekiah. — R. C. Sproul, *The Holiness of God* (Wheaton, IL: Tyndale House Publishers, 1993), 25–26.

12. What do we know about Uzziah?

The record of the call of Isaiah is perhaps the most dramatic of all such calls recorded for us in the Old Testament. We are told that it came to pass in the year that King Uzziah died.

King Uzziah died in the eighth century B.C. His reign was important in Jewish history. He was one of the better kings who ruled over Judah. He was not a David, but neither was he noted for the corruption that characterized the kings of the north such as Ahab. Uzziah ascended to the throne when he was sixteen years old. He reigned in Jerusalem for fifty-two years. Think of it, fifty-two years! In the past fifty-two years the United States has witnessed the administrations of Roosevelt, Truman, Eisenhower, Kennedy, Johnson, Nixon, Ford, Carter, and Reagan. But many people in Jerusalem lived their entire lives under the reign of King Uzziah.

The Bible tells us that Uzziah began his reign in godliness, doing "what was right in the sight of the

Lord." He sought after God and God blessed him. He was victorious in battle over the Philistines and other nations. He built towers in Jerusalem and strengthened the city walls. He dug massive cisterns in the desert and stimulated great expansion in the nation's agriculture. He restored the military power of Judah to a standard almost as high as it had been under David. For most of his career Uzziah was noted as a great and beloved king.

The story of Uzziah ends with a sad note. The last years of his life were like those of a Shakespearian tragic hero. His career was marred by the sin of pride committed after he acquired great wealth and power. He tried to play God. He boldly entered the temple and arrogantly claimed for himself the rights that God had given only to the priests. When the priests of the temple tried to stop his act of sacrilege, Uzziah became enraged. While he was screaming at them in fury, leprosy broke out on his forehead. The Bible says of him:

> He lived in a separate house—being a leper ... cut off from the house of the Lord. (2 Chronicles 26:21, NASB) — R. C. Sproul, *The Holiness of God* (Wheaton, IL: Tyndale House Publishers, 1993), 27–28.

13. What would have been the mood of the country in the year that King Uzziah died?

When Uzziah died, in spite of the shame of his later years, it was a time of national mourning. Isaiah went to the temple, presumably looking for consolation in a time of national and personal grief. He got more than he bargained for:

> In the year the King Uzziah died I saw also the Lord sitting upon a throne, high and lifted up, and his train [of his robe] filled the temple. (Isaiah 6:1)

The king was dead. But when Isaiah entered the temple he saw another king, the Ultimate King, the One who sat forever on the throne of Judah. He saw the Lord. — R. C. Sproul, *The Holiness of God* (Wheaton, IL: Tyndale House Publishers, 1993), 28–29.

14. Compare "Lord" in verses 1 and 3. Why is it in all caps in one case and not in the other?

Notice how in Isaiah 6:1 the word Lord is printed. It begins with a capital letter and then is finished with lowercase letters. This stands in contrast with the word LORD that occurs later in the text and frequently in Scripture. Sometimes the word Lord appears in all capital letters—LORD. This is not an error in printing or a mere inconsistency on the part of the translator. Most English translations of the Bible follow this device of rendering the word Lord sometimes in lowercase letters and other times in uppercase letters. The reason for this difference is that two different Hebrew words are used in the original text, but both are rendered in English by the word Lord.

When the word Lord occurs in lowercase letters, the translator is indicating to us that the word Adonai is found in the Hebrew Bible. Adonai means "sovereign one." It is not the name of God. It is a title for God, indeed the supreme title given to God in the Old Testament. When LORD appears in all capital letters it indicates that the word Jahweh is used in the Old Testament. Jahweh is the sacred name of God, the name God revealed Himself to Moses with in the burning bush. This is the unspeakable name, the ineffable name, the holy name that is guarded from profanity in the life of Israel. Normally it occurs only with the use of its four consonants—yhwh. It is therefore referred to as the sacred "tetragrammaton," the unspeakable four letters. — R. C. Sproul, *The Holiness of God* (Wheaton, IL: Tyndale House Publishers, 1993), 29–30.

15. In the year that King Uzziah died, I saw the Lord... How common was this?

When Isaiah came to the temple, there was a crisis of sovereignty in the land. Uzziah was dead. The eyes of Isaiah were opened to see the real King of the nation. He saw God seated on the throne, the sovereign one.

Men are not allowed to see the face of God. The Scriptures warn that no man can see God and live. We remember Moses' request when he ascended into the holy mountain of God. Moses had been an eyewitness of astonishing miracles. He had heard the voice of God speaking to him out of the burning bush. He had witnessed the river Nile turn into blood. He had tasted manna from heaven and gazed upon the pillar of cloud and the pillar of fire. He had seen the chariots of Pharaoh inundated by the waves of the Red Sea. Still he was not satisfied. He wanted more. He craved the ultimate spiritual experience. He inquired of the Lord on the mountain, "Let me see your face. Show me your glory." The request was denied:

> And the LORD said, "I will cause all my goodness to pass in front of you, and I will proclaim my name, the LORD in your presence. I will have mercy on whom I will have mercy, and I will have compassion on whom I will have compassion. But," he said, "you cannot see my face, for no one may see me and live." Then the LORD said, "There is a place near me where you may stand on a rock. When my glory passes by, I will put you in a cleft in the rock and cover you with my hand until I have passed by. Then I will remove

my hand and you will see my back; but my face must not be seen." (Exodus 33:19–23, NIV)

— R. C. Sproul, *The Holiness of God* (Wheaton, IL: Tyndale House Publishers, 1993), 31–32.

16. As Christians, are we allowed to see what Moses could not see—the glory of God?

If people are terrified by the sight of the reflected glory of the back parts of God, how can anyone stand to gaze directly into His holy face?

Yet the final goal of every Christian is to be allowed to see what was denied to Moses. We want to see Him face to face. We want to bask in the radiant glory of His divine countenance. It was the hope of every Jew, a hope instilled in the most famous and beloved benediction of Israel:

> The LORD bless thee and keep thee: The LORD make his face shine upon thee, and be gracious unto thee: The LORD lift up his countenance upon thee and give thee peace. (Numbers 6:24–26)

This hope, crystallized in the benediction of Israel, becomes more than a hope for the Christian—it becomes a promise. St. John tells in his first letter:

> Now are we the sons of God, and it doth not yet appear what we shall be: but we know that, when he shall appear, we shall be like him, for we shall see him as he is. (1 John 3:2)

Here is the promise of God: We shall see Him as He is. Theologians call this future expectation the Beatific Vision. We will see God as He is. This means that someday we will see God face to face. We will not see the reflected glory of a burning bush or a pillar of cloud.

We will see Him as He is, as He is in His pure divine essence. — R. C. Sproul, *The Holiness of God* (Wheaton, IL: Tyndale House Publishers, 1993), 33–34.

17. Why is "Holy" repeated three times?

The significance of the repetition of the word holy can be easily missed. It represents a peculiar literary device that is found in Hebrew forms of literature, especially in poetry. The repetition is a form of emphasis. When we want to emphasize the importance of something in English we have several devices to choose from. We may underline the important words or print them in italics or boldface type. We may attach an exclamation point following the words or set them off in quotation marks. These are all devices to call the reader's attention to something that is especially important.

The Old Testament Jew also had different techniques to indicate emphasis. One such device was the method of repetition. We see Jesus' use of repetition with the words, "Truly, truly, I say unto you...." Here the double use of truly was a sign that what He was about to say was of crucial importance. The word translated "truly" is the ancient word amen. We normally think of the word amen as something people say at the end of a sermon or of a prayer. It means simply, "It is true." Jesus used it as a preface instead of a response.

A humorous use of the repetition device may be seen in Genesis 14. The story of the battle of the kings in the Valley of Siddim mentions men who fell in the great tar pits of the region. Some translators call them asphalt pits, or bitumen pits, or simply great pits. Why the confusion in translation? Exactly what kind of pits were they? The Hebrew is unclear. The original text gives the Hebrew word for pit and then simply repeats it. The story speaks literally of pit pits. The Jew was saying that there are pits and there are pits. Some pits are pittier than other pits. These pits—the pit pits—were the pittiest pits of all. It is one thing to fall into a pit. But if you fall into a pit pit you are in deep trouble.

On a handful of occasions the Bible repeats something to the third degree. To mention something three times in succession is to elevate it to the superlative degree, to attach to it emphasis of super importance. — R. C. Sproul, *The Holiness of God* (Wheaton, IL: Tyndale House Publishers, 1993), 37–38.

18. What is the lesson for us in this story? What is the application? How does it change our view of God?

A recent survey of ex-church members revealed that the main reason they stopped going to church was that they found it boring. It is difficult for many people to find worship a thrilling and moving experience. We note here, when God appeared in the temple, the doors and the thresholds were moved. The inert matter of doorposts, the inanimate thresholds, the wood and metal that could neither hear nor speak had the good sense to be moved by the presence of God. The literal meaning of the text is that they were shaken. They began to quake where they stood.

"Woe to me!" I cried. "I am ruined! For I am a man of unclean lips, and I live among a people of unclean lips, and my eyes have seen the King, the LORD Almighty." (Isaiah 6:5, NIV)

The doors of the temple were not the only things that were shaking. The thing that quaked the most in the building was the body of Isaiah. When he saw the living God, the reigning monarch of the universe displayed before his eyes in all of His holiness, Isaiah cried out,

"Woe is me!" — R. C. Sproul, *The Holiness of God* (Wheaton, IL: Tyndale House Publishers, 1993), 39–40.

19. What did you learn to day? What do you want to remember?

20. How can we pray for each other this week?

Not God Enough, Lesson #4
Chapter #6: One Choice
Chapter #7: You Don't Get Your Own Personal Jesus
Good Questions Have Groups Talking
www.joshhunt.com

OPEN:

What is one thing you are grateful for today?

DIG

1. **Exodus 3. Moses and the burning bush. Think of the context of this story. What question might Moses have had for God? Think of Moses life, and the status of God's people at this point.**

   Moses had a miraculous birth story he had, no doubt, heard many times growing up. Yet, when he stepped up and tried to help his people, nothing good came of it. For the last forty years, he has been wandering around the desert tending sheep.

   The people of God also had a miraculous birth story. Yet, for the last 400 years they have lived in slavery. Among other things, Moses might want to ask: Where are you, God? Why do you let bad things happen to your people?

2. Exodus 3.14. What answer did God provide Moses?

Do we value God for who He is, or do we value him like a farmer values his cow? Just for the milk and the cheese? Do we love God like kids love the ice cream man? Is it just about the stuff He provides? Just about what He can do for us?

If so, what happens when the milk runs dry and the ice cream man's truck breaks down? What do you do when you find yourself hundreds of miles away from home, your hopes and dreams shattered? What if those dreams were even good dreams about serving God?

At times like that, you need a faith in the God who is actually there, the kind of God who says, "If you're looking for God, I AM the God you get, because I AM who I AM."

And that will have to be enough. — Kenneth Boa and John Turner, *The 52 Greatest Stories of the Bible: A Devotional Study* (Grand Rapids, MI: Baker Books, 2008).

3. John 8.58 – 59. Jesus picks up on this, "I am" language. What does Jesus reveal about Himself here?

Jesus was claiming deity in this statement. The statement "I am," Ego amimni, is a unique expression whereby Jesus identifies with the Lord (Jehovah) of the Old Testament. Just as the root meaning of Lord is "I am, I am," Jesus came identifying Himself with God when He said, "I am light, I am bread, I am vine . . ." When Jesus said, "Before Abraham was, I am," He was equating Himself with deity. His opponents picking up stones to kill Him for blasphemy demonstrates they understood what Jesus meant. — Elmer Towns, *Bible Answers for*

Almost All Your Questions (Nashville: Thomas Nelson, 2003).

4. **Who did Jesus claim to be?**

   He claimed to be Jehovah (Yahweh)
   He claimed to be equal with God
   He claimed to be Messiah God
   He claimed this by accepting worship
   He claimed to have equal authority with God
   He claimed this by requesting prayer in His name
   What claims did Jesus' disciples make about Him?
   They attributed to Jesus the titles of deity
   They considered Him to be Messiah—God
   They attributed the powers of God to Jesus
   They associated Jesus' name with God's
   They called Him God directly
   They said He was superior to angels

   Norman L. Geisler and Ronald M. Brooks, *When Skeptics Ask* (Wheaton, IL: Victor Books, 1990), 289.

5. **Lewis famously said that Jesus was either Liar, Lord, or Lunatic. Here is the exact quote from *Mere Christianity*." I am trying here to prevent anyone saying the really foolish thing that people often say about Him: 'I'm ready to accept Jesus as a great moral teacher, but I don't accept His claim to be God.' That is the one thing we must not say. A man who was merely a man and said the sort of things Jesus said would not be a great moral teacher. He would either be a lunatic—on a level with the man who says he is a poached egg—or else he would be the Devil of Hell. You must make your choice. Either this man was, and is, the Son of God: or else a madman or something worse. You can shut Him up for a fool, you can spit at Him and kill Him as a demon; or you can fall at His feet and call Him Lord**

and God. But let us not come with any patronising nonsense about His being a great human teacher. He has not left that open to us. He did not intend to." What does Lewis have in mind in the phrase, "said the sort of thing that Jesus said"?

Let's take a look at how Jesus identifies Himself throughout His life. In John 14:6, He says, "I am the way and the truth and the life. No one comes to the Father except through me."

Leading up to Jesus' crucifixion, He was taken before Caiaphas, the Jewish high priest, for a trial. In chapter 14 of Mark's account, we read that many people were testifying falsely against Jesus in front of Caiaphas, and Jesus remained silent. Finally, Caiaphas asked Jesus, "Are you the Messiah, the Son of the Blessed One?" and Jesus answered, "I am. . . . And you will see the Son of Man sitting at the right hand of the Mighty One and coming on the clouds of heaven" (vv. 61–62). Jesus' answer so offended Caiaphas that he tore his clothes and declared Jesus guilty of blasphemy, a crime punishable by death.

Why was Jesus calling Himself the "Son of Man" so shocking? First, Jesus answered Caiaphas by affirming that He was the Messiah, the Savior. But the title "Son of Man" has a very specific meaning. Yes, He was a human being, a son of man, but in Daniel 7 the title of "Son of Man" is given to the exalted heavenly One who will rule heaven, and that is why Jesus uses that name for Himself. He will save men from their sins, giving them eternal life, and be the exalted One who reigns forever over the kingdom of heaven. — Chip Ingram, *Why I Believe: Straight Answers to Honest Questions about God, the Bible, and Christianity* (Grand Rapids, MI: Baker Books, 2017).

6. **Everything hinges on this: was Jesus who He said He was. Strong evidence comes from fulfilled prophecy. One good example is Isaiah 53. Look over this chapter silently. What fulfilled prophecy do you see in this chapter?**

53:1 One would think that a terminally ill world would gladly embrace the cure of the gospel, but few, so few, believe our report (see John 12:38–40).

53:3 The ungodly still despise and reject the name of Jesus Christ. It is used worldwide as a cuss word to express disgust. Adolf Hitler's name wasn't despised enough to use in such a way.

53:7 Pilate marveled at the silence of God's Lamb (see Matthew 27:12–14).

53:9 See Matthew 27:57–60. Also see 1 Peter 2:22.

53:10 See 2 Corinthians 5:21.

53:11 See 1 John 2:1, Isaiah 42:1 and Romans 5:15–18.

53:12 See Psalm 2:8, Colossians 2:15, Isaiah 50:6, Romans 3:25, Matthew 27:38, Mark 15:28, Luke 22:37 and 2 Corinthians 5:21.

— Ray Comfort, *The Evidence Bible: Irrefutable Evidence for the Thinking Mind, Notes, ed. Kirk Cameron, The Way of the Master Evidence Bible* (Orlando, FL: Bridge-Logos, 2003).

7. **Can you think of other fulfilled prophecies?**

Old Testament prophecies about Jesus' birth

Prophesied	Fulfilled

1	Born as a descendant of a woman, *Genesis 3:15*	Galatians 4:4
2	Born of a virgin, *Isaiah 7:14*	Matthew 1:18–25
3	Born as a descendant of David, *Jeremiah 23:5*	Luke 3:31
4	Born in Bethlehem, *Micah 5:2*	Matthew 2:1–6
5.	Herod kills the children, *Jeremiah 31:15*	Matthew 2:16–18

Old Testament prophecies about Jesus' death

	Prophesied	**Fulfilled**
1	Betrayed by a friend, *Psalm 41:9*	*John 13:18–27*
2	Sold for 30 pieces of silver, *Zechariah 11:12*	*Matthew 26:14–15*
3	Forsaken by his disciples, *Zechariah 13:7*	*Mark 14:27, 50*
4	Accused by false witnesses, *Psalm 35:11, 20–21*	*Matthew 26:59–61*
5	Silent before accusers, *Isaiah 53:7*	*Matthew 27:12–14*
6	Wounded and bruised, *Isaiah 53:4–6*	*1 Peter 2:21–25*
7	Beaten and spat on, *Isaiah 50:6*	*Matthew 26:67–68*
8	Mocked, *Psalm 22:6–8*	*Matthew 27:27–31*
9	Hands and feet pierced, *Psalm 22:16*	*John 20:24–28*
10	Crucified with thieves, *Isaiah 53:12*	*Matthew 27:38*

11	Prayed for his enemies, *Isaiah 53:12*	*Luke 23:34*
12	People shake their heads, *Psalm 22:7; 109:25*	*Matthew 27:39*
13	Cloths gambled for, *Psalm 22:18*	*John 19:23–24*
14	Became very thirsty, *Psalm 22:15*	*John 19:28*
15	Gall and vinegar offered to him, *Psalm 69:21*	*Matthew 27:34*
16	His forsaken cry, *Psalm 22:1*	*Matthew 27:46*
17	Committed himself to God, *Psalm 31:5*	*Luke 23:46*
18	Bones not broken, *Psalm 34:20*	*John 19:32–36*
19	His side pierced, *Zechariah 12:10*	*John 19:34, 37*
20	Buried in rich man's tomb, *Isaiah 53:9*	*Matthew 27:57–60*

Mark Water, *Hard Questions about the Bible Made Easy*, The Made Easy Series (Alresford, Hampshire: John Hunt Publishers Ltd, 2000), 30.

8. What are the odds that Jesus could fulfil these prophecies?

The Bible contains hundreds of detailed prophecies.

Over 60 prophecies in the Old Testament are distinct predictions about Jesus.

Some of these prophecies were made 1,000 years before Jesus lived his life on earth.

Many of these prophecies concern Jesus' crucifixion. These prophecies were made over 500 years before crucifixion was first used anywhere in the world as a form of capital punishment.

Could it just be a fluke that Jesus fulfilled all these prophecies?

A scientist picked out 48 such prophecies and determined that the probability of one man randomly fulfilling them all is 1 in 10 to the exponent of 157. That is 1 followed by 157 zeros!

10,000,000,000,000,000,000,000,000,000,000,000, 000,000,000,000,000,000,000, 000,000,000,000,000,00 0,000,000,000,000,000,000,000,000,000,000,000,000,0 00,000, 000,000,000,000,000,000,000,000,000,000,000, 000,000 — Mark Water, *Hard Questions about the Bible Made Easy, The Made Easy Series* (Alresford, Hampshire: John Hunt Publishers Ltd, 2000), 30.

9. **1 Corinthians 15.12ff. Look over this passage silently. Why is the resurrection central to the Christian faith? Why is the Christian faith impossible without the resurrection?**

According to the apostle Paul, if the bodily resurrection of Jesus Christ isn't true, Christianity is a hoax, and it's a bad one, and none of it is true.

Despite the centuries of skepticism and criticism, the truth remains that the resurrection of Jesus Christ is central to the Christian faith. Both Christians and atheists agree that Jesus' resurrection from the dead is vital.

Prominent atheist professor of philosophy Antony Flew and Christian professor of apologetics and philosophy Gary Habermas began debating in 1985.

Over the next two decades, their debates led to several books, including Did Jesus Rise from the Dead? The Resurrection Debate. In this book, Flew writes,

First, we [Habermas and myself] both construe resurrection, or the rising from the dead, in a thoroughly literal and physical way. . . .

Second, we are again agreed that the question whether, in that literal understanding, Jesus did rise from the dead is of supreme theoretical and practical importance. For the knowable fact that he did, if it is indeed a knowable fact, is the best, if not the only, reason for accepting that Jesus is the God of Abraham, Isaac, and Israel.

Third, we are agreed both that the identification is the defining and distinguishing characteristic of the true Christian, and that it is scarcely possible to make it without also accepting that the Resurrection did literally happen.1

What Flew is saying is, if Jesus rose, you have an intellectually feasible argument that everything Jesus said could be true. If he didn't, all of Christianity falls. — Chip Ingram, *Why I Believe: Straight Answers to Honest Questions about God, the Bible*, and Christianity (Grand Rapids, MI: Baker Books, 2017).

Chapter #7: You Don't Get Your Own Personal Jesus

10. John 14.6. What does Jesus reveal about Himself in this classic verse?

Jesus' words in John 14:6 are what separate Christianity from every other religion in the world. For that reason, they're also probably some of the most controversial sentences in all Scripture.

Few people like to be told that there's only one way to do something. The natural response is to disagree and offer several alternatives. That's certainly what happens when talk turns to religion. When Jesus says, "No one comes to the Father except through me," many people say, "Oh, yeah? What about Islam and Buddhism and Hinduism?" They don't like the idea of one group of people having exclusive rights to heaven. And they especially don't like the idea of one group believing that they are right and everyone else is wrong. That's why spiritual discussions often turn into heated debates or shouting matches.

As Christians, we should be aware of people's feelings about this topic, but we should never back away from the truth of John 14:6. We should learn to present the truth in a way that invites discussion instead of argument. And we should always be prepared to explain why Jesus, and Jesus alone, is the way to salvation. — Christopher D. Hudson, *Niv, Once-a-Day: At the Table Family Devotional, Ebook* (Grand Rapids, MI: Zondervan, 2012).

11. Can you think of other verses where Jesus made similar exclusive claims?

This is the sixth of Jesus' seven famous "I am" sayings, each of which is radically exclusive in setting Jesus apart as the one and only Savior. In each of these statements, Jesus uses the word the rather than a. He is "the bread of life" (John 6:35), not a bread of life: that is, Jesus is the one and only source of satisfaction for the hunger of our souls. Likewise, Jesus is "the light of the world" (8:12), the only guide who can lead mankind out of darkness into the light of God. Jesus said, "I am the door" (10:7), since through him alone we can enter the fold of God, and "I am the good shepherd" (10:11), who alone lays down his life for the sheep. To these, Jesus added the remarkable statement, "I am the resurrection and the life" (11:25), claiming to be the Conqueror even of death—a claim that he backed up by raising Lazarus from the grave (11:43–44). Each of these statements is radically exclusive, asserting that none but Jesus can save us from sin, bring us to God, and grant us eternal life.

This same focus on the person of Jesus is seen all through this portion of John's Gospel, which centers on four questions asked by the disciples, each of which Jesus answered by directing them to himself. Peter asked, "Lord, where are you going?" (John 13:36). Thomas continued, "How can we know the way?" (14:5). Philip added, "Lord, show us the Father" (14:8), and Judas (not the betrayer) asked, "Lord, how is it that you will manifest yourself to us, and not to the world?" (14:22). These are slightly different questions, and each receives a slightly different answer. But each of the answers is a variant on John 14:6: "I am the way, and the truth, and the life." — Richard D. Phillips, *John*, ed. Richard D. Phillips, Philip Graham Ryken, and Daniel M. Doriani, *1st ed., vol. 2, Reformed Expository Commentary* (Phillipsburg, NJ: P&R Publishing, 2014), 203–204.

12. Perhaps you have heard people say, "Jesus is fine for you; I am just not into that kind of thing." You say?

One modern critic has spouted contempt for Christianity's exclusivity in these words: "Christianity is a contentious faith which requires an all-or-nothing commitment to Jesus as the one and only incarnation of the Son of God." We can endorse this author's assessment, though not perhaps all that he goes on to say: "[Christians are] uncompromising, ornery, militant, rigorous, imperious and invincibly self-righteous." This is not a recent opinion of our faith: Philip Ryken asserts that "for the past 2,000 years, Christianity's claims about the unique truth of Jesus Christ have aroused no end of opposition from Jews, pagans, Muslims, Communists, humanists, and atheists."2

We might think this opposition to have lessened with the advent of post-modernity, given its emphasis on tolerance. Instead, the opposite has happened. Postmodern unbelievers grant tolerance to every religion except Christianity, precisely because the gospel is seen as the ultimate intolerant creed. The gospel's message that only Jesus can save offends postmodernity's relativist mantra, since Christians insist that all other religions are false and any other route to God is a dead end. Objections to these doctrines have marked the world's hatred for Jesus ever since he spoke the words that John's Gospel continues to proclaim today: "I am the way, and the truth, and the life" (John 14:6). — Richard D. Phillips, *John*, ed. Richard D. Phillips, Philip Graham Ryken, and Daniel M. Doriani, *1st ed., vol. 2, Reformed Expository Commentary* (Phillipsburg, NJ: P&R Publishing, 2014), 202–203.

13. Think about it for a moment. Why does the popular notion of, "Many paths lead to God" not make any sense?

Suppose you are at the intersection of a busy city street and a stranger walks up to you and asks directions to the city hall. What would happen if your response went something like this:

"Friend, there is no one true way to get to city hall. Everyone must find their own way. You see, we stand at the intersection of four possible roadways. Beyond this intersection are countless others. You must choose the path that leads to city hall, because only you can walk that path. No one else may choose it for you. Good luck on your journey."

The stranger would probably think that you had escaped from the mental ward of a local hospital. However, this is the same lunacy that we hear from postmodern thinkers who declare that everyone must find their own way to God. I would suggest that God is more "real" than city hall and that finding our way back to Him requires definite instruction. Thankfully for us, God has taken the initiative by coming into the world through Jesus Christ, to point out the way back home to Himself. Jesus knew exactly what He was talking about when He said, "I am the way and the truth and the life. No one comes to the Father except through me" (John 14:6). == Terry A. Bowland, *Make Disciples: Reaching the Postmodern World for Christ* (Joplin, MO: College Press Publishing, 1999), 216–217.

14. Critics say that Christians are bigoted and narrow-minded. You say?

The Bible declares plainly that without Christ, we are without God's promises; without Christ, we are without hope; without Christ, we are without God; without Christ, we are lost ... lost forever.

At this point, many today balk at the teachings of the church. "Do you mean to say," they ask, "that all those outside the church have no hope whatsoever? What about all the sincere folks who never come to Christ? What of the billions in the worlds of Islam, Buddhism and Hinduism? What of those who have never heard? What of my neighbors and friends who are good-hearted people, but who have never made Christ their Lord and Savior? Are you saying that they are lost? Why, if that's true, then this 'gospel' has made you Christians the most narrow-minded, bigoted people on the face of the earth."

At first, it appears difficult to respond to such claims. Perhaps, we should reply by saying, that far from being narrow-minded and bigoted, Christians are, in fact, the most loving people in the world.

Suppose you are a doctor and an individual comes to you one day and describes his symptoms. After taking a blood test you realize that this fellow has acute diabetes. You prescribe insulin injections. "Insulin!" he cries. "I don't want to take insulin." You assure him that he must take insulin.

"But, I don't want to take insulin," he complains. "Can't I take some other drug. How about penicillin? How about a double dose of Tylenol? Won't those do?" Again you reaffirm that without the insulin, he will die.

Then he exclaims, "Why, doctor, I believe you are the most narrow, closed-minded, bigoted physician I have ever met." Now, here's the question: Is the doctor narrow and bigoted or is the doctor loving, because he is telling the man the truth—the only truth which will give him life!

Christians are not narrow or bigoted. Christians are loving because we declare to the world the truth. In our sin, we are at war with God, without hope, without God in the world. But Jesus is our solution. The gospel of Christ brings us peace with God. There is no peace that can be purchased on the bargain counter. Only through Christ's victory on the cross where God justly punishes sin and mercifully pardons the sinner, only there do we find that which brings peace. "He is our peace!" This isn't narrow or bigoted. It is the truth! — Terry A.

Bowland, *Make Disciples: Reaching the Postmodern World for Christ* (Joplin, MO: College Press Publishing, 1999), 48–49.

15. Exodus 20.4. We don't ever do this, right?

What does the word idolatry suggest to your mind? Savages groveling before a totem pole? Cruel-faced statues in Hindu temples? The dervish dance of the priests of Baal around Elijah's altar? These things are certainly idolatrous, in a very obvious way, but we need to realize that there are more subtle forms of idolatry as well.

Look at the second commandment. It runs as follows, "You shall not make for yourself an idol in the form of anything in heaven above or on the earth beneath or in the waters below. You shall not bow down to them or worship them; for I, the LORD your God, am a jealous God" (Ex 20:4-5). What is this commandment talking about?

If it stood alone, it would be natural to suppose that it refers to the worship of images of gods other than Jehovah—the Babylonian idol worship, for instance, which Isaiah derided (Is 44:9-20; 46:67), or the paganism of the Greco-Roman world of Paul's day, of which he wrote in

Romans 1:23, 25 that they "exchanged the glory of the immortal God for images made to look like mortal man and birds and animals and reptiles. . . They exchanged the truth of God for a 'lie, and worshiped and served created things rather than the Creator." But in its context the second commandment can hardly be referring to this sort of idolatry, for if it were it would simply be repeating the thought of the first commandment without adding anything to it.

Accordingly, we take the second commandment—as in fact it has always been taken—as pointing us to the principle that (to quote Charles Hodge) "idolatry consists not only in the worship of false gods, but also in the worship of the true God by images." In its Christian application, this means that we are not to make use of visual or pictorial representations of the triune God, or of any person of the Trinity, for the purposes of Christian worship. The commandment thus deals not with the object of our worship, but with the manner of it, what it tells us is that statues and pictures of the One whom we worship are not to be used as an aid to worshiping him.
— J.I. Packer, *Knowing God*, 1973.

16. What is the big deal with using an image to help you worship the one true God?

It may seem strange at first sight that such a prohibition should find a place among the ten basic principles of biblical religion, for at first sight it does not seem to have much point. What harm is there, we ask, in the worshiper's surrounding himself with statues and pictures, if they help him to lift his heart to God?

We are accustomed to treating the question of whether these things should be used or not as a matter of temperament and personal taste. We know that some people have crucifixes and pictures of Christ in their rooms, and they tell us that looking at these objects helps them to focus their thoughts on Christ when they pray. We know that many claim to be able to worship more freely and easily in churches that are filled with such ornaments than they can in churches that are bare of them. Well, we say, what is wrong with that? What harm can these things do? If people really do find them helpful, what more is there to be said? What point can there be in prohibiting them? In the face of this perplexity, some would suggest that the second commandment applies only to immoral and degrading representations of God, borrowed from pagan cults, and to nothing more.

But the very wording of the commandment rules out such a limiting exposition. God says quite categorically, "Thou shalt not make any likeness of any thing" for use in worship. This categorical statement rules out not simply the use of pictures and statues which depict God as an animal, but also the use of pictures and statues which depict him as the highest created thing we know-a human. It also rules out the use of pictures and statues of Jesus Christ as a man, although Jesus himself was and remains man; for all pictures and statues are necessarily made after the "likeness" of ideal manhood as we conceive it, and therefore come under the ban which the commandment imposes. — J.I. Packer, *Knowing God*, 1973.

17. Does this mean that we should not use images of Jesus in teaching about Jesus?

Historically, Christians have differed as to whether the second commandment forbids the use of pictures of Jesus for purposes of teaching and instruction (in Sunday-school classes, for instance), and the question is not an easy one to settle; but there is no room for doubting that the commandment obliges us to dissociate our worship, both in public and in private, from all pictures and statues of Christ, no less than from pictures and statues of his Father. — J.I. Packer, *Knowing God*, 1973.

18. **Imagine a friend said that images helped him or her feel close to God—just as the Bible does or going to church does. What's the harm? You say?**

Images dishonor God, for they obscure his glory. The likeness of things in heaven (sun, moon, stars), and in earth (people, animals, birds, insects), and in the sea (fish, mammals, crustaceans), is precisely not a likeness of their Creator. "A true image of God," wrote Calvin, "is not to be found in all the world; and hence. . . His glory is defiled, and His truth corrupted by the lie, whenever He is set before our eyes in a visible form. . . Therefore, to devise any image of God is itself impious; because by this corruption His majesty is adulterated, and. He is figured to be other than He is."

The point here is not just that an image represents God as having body and parts, whereas in reality he has neither. If this were the only ground of objection to images, representations of Christ would be blameless. But the point really goes much deeper. The heart of the objection to pictures and images is that they inevitably conceal most, if not all, of the truth about the personal nature and character of the divine Being whom they represent.

To illustrate: Aaron made a golden calf (that is, a bull-image). It was meant as a visible symbol of Jehovah, the mighty God who had brought Israel out of Egypt. No doubt the image was thought to honor him, as being a fitting symbol of his great strength. But it is not hard to see that such a symbol in fact insults him, for what idea of his moral character, his righteousness, goodness and patience could one gather from looking at a statue of him as a bull? Thus Aaron's image hid Jehovah's glory.

In a similar way, the pathos of the crucifix obscures the glory of Christ, for it hides the fact of his deity, his victory on the cross, and his present kingdom. It displays his human weakness, but it conceals his divine strength; it depicts the reality of his pain, but keeps out of our sight the reality of his joy and his power. In both these cases, the symbol is unworthy most of all because of what it fails to display. And so are all other visible representations of deity.

Whatever we may think of religious art from a cultural standpoint, we should not look to pictures of God to show us his glory and move us to worship; for his glory is precisely what such pictures can never show us. And this is why God added to the second commandment a reference to himself as "jealous" to avenge himself on those who disobey him: for God's "jealousy" in the Bible is his zeal to maintain his own glory, which is jeopardized when images are used in worship. — J.I. Packer, *Knowing God*, 1973.

19. What do you want to remember from our conversation today?

20. How can we pray for one another?

Not God Enough, Lesson #5
Chapter #8: The God We Crave
Good Questions Have Groups Talking
www.joshhunt.com

OPEN:

Opening question: did you lose anything this week?

DIG

1. **Greear starts this week's chapter with these words: I am missing something. Ever feel this way? Who has a story?**

   You've probably heard the axiom, "There is a God-shaped vacuum in the heart of every man." The saying is often attributed to Blaise Pascal, the seventeenth-century mathematician, physicist, inventor, and Catholic philosopher. What he actually wrote is even more eloquent:

   > What else does this craving [in man], and this helplessness, proclaim but that there was once in man a true happiness, of which all that now remains is the empty print and trace? This he tries in vain to fill with everything around him, seeking in things that are not there the help he cannot find in those that are, though none can help, since this infinite abyss can be filled only with an infinite and immutable object, in other words with God himself.

The God-shaped vacuum longs to be filled with its missing part. Ask yourself: "Am I missing that part? Have I so successfully filled the vacuum with God-substitutes that I've left little room for Him? If so, what have I stuffed in that vacuum? Is all that stuff working for me? Are all those things enough? Could God bring more satisfaction than they do? If I make more room for God, would I have to give up all these other things? Is there room in there for both? What things would need to go and what could remain? How would those that remain align with God?" — Steve Silver, *New Man Journey: Finding Meaning in Retirement* (Colorado Springs, CO: David C Cook, 2013).

2. Jeremiah 2.13. What do we learn about sin from this passage?

Jesus said that rivers of living water would flow out of the lives of those who believe in Him. His living water would brim over from the wellspring of the Spirit within us, quenching our thirst and touching the parched lives of those around us. The life of the Lord Jesus is a constantly flowing stream, a river even, keeping us fresh, filled, and satisfied.

We stop the flow, however, when we try to reservoir God's spring of living water in our lives. We become cisterns—holding tanks for past victories or other people's ideas. At that point, we have forsaken the spring of living water. We have tried to store that which cannot be saved, we have tried to keep that which must keep flowing. The result? Our lives lack freshness and freedom, and we become stagnant pools reflecting old experiences and tired testimonies.

God says that these cisterns of our own making will break. What we try to save, we will lose. The warning is clear: Throw out the broken cisterns and get in the flow of God's spring of living water.

If you know anything about springs and cisterns, this warning in Jeremiah 2:13 should be easy to grasp. A spring is a flow of water from the ground, often a source of a stream. A cistern is a large receptacle for storing water. Don't rely on yesterday's experiences or last month's victories. God wants to give you fresh, thirst-quenching life each new day. So start with this prayer...

Jesus, the Living Water, I thirst after You. May Your life in me not be a trickle, or even a small stream but a river. I confess my sin, clearing away any obstruction that might hinder Your flow in my life. — Joni Eareckson Tada, *Diamonds in the Dust: 366 Sparkling Devotions* (Grand Rapids, MI: Zondervan, 2010).

3. Just to be clear… what is a cistern?

Cisterns are wells that are dug into the earth, usually into solid rock, with the intention of holding water. God is painting a fascinating word picture in these words of the prophet. He is saying, "You have rejected Me as a fountain of living water for your life." A fountain is an artesian spring—one that bubbles up from the earth with an unending supply of fresh, pure water. A fountain gives water that is free for the asking. — Charles F. Stanley, *Experiencing Forgiveness* (Nashville: T. Nelson Publishers, 1996).

4. Does this remind you of anything Jesus said? See if you can find it on your phone app.

Jesus encountered a Samaritan woman by the well of Sychar, and in the course of His conversation with her, He said of Himself, "If you knew the gift of God, and who it is who says to you, 'Give Me a drink,' you would have asked Him, and He would have given you living water" (John 4:10). Jesus is painting this same word picture about Himself—He has life to give that is eternal and is freely offered. His forgiveness—and the eternal life associated with it—is a fountain from which we can draw in an unending fashion. His forgiveness is free for the asking.

"But," God says through Jeremiah, "instead of choosing My living water, you have chosen to build cisterns." To build is an act of the will. The cistern builders rejected the artesian spring for a well of their own making. And the Lord noted with sadness but with certainty, "It is a broken well." There is a crack in the cistern, which means that it won't hold the water. — Charles F. Stanley, *Experiencing Forgiveness* (Nashville: T. Nelson Publishers, 1996).

5. **Although worship is not mentioned in this verse, John Piper finds a rich lesson about worship that he often quotes. See if you can find it.**

I conclude from this meditation on the nature of worship that the revolt against hedonism has killed the spirit of worship in many churches and many hearts. The widespread notion that high moral acts must be free from self-interest is a great enemy of true worship. Worship is the highest moral act a human can perform, so the only basis and motivation for it that many people can conceive is the notion of morality as the disinterested performance of duty. But when worship is reduced to disinterested duty, it ceases to be worship. For worship is a feast.

Neither God nor my wife is honored when I celebrate the high days of our relationship out of a sense of duty. They are honored when I delight in them! Therefore, to honor God in worship, we must not seek Him disinterestedly for fear of gaining some joy in worship and so ruining the moral value of the act. Instead we must seek Him hedonistically, the way a thirsty deer seeks the stream—precisely for the joy of seeing and knowing Him! Worship is nothing less than obedience to the command of God: "Delight yourself in the LORD"!

Misguided virtue smothers the spirit of worship. The person who has the vague notion that it is virtue to overcome self-interest, and that it is vice to seek pleasure, will scarcely be able to worship. For worship is the most hedonistic affair of life and must not be ruined with the least thought of disinterestedness. The great hindrance to worship is not that we are a pleasure-seeking people, but that we are willing to settle for such pitiful pleasures.

The prophet Jeremiah put it like this:

> "My people have changed their glory for that which does not profit. Be appalled, O heavens, at this; be shocked, be utterly desolate, declares the LORD, for my people have committed two evils: they have forsaken me, the fountain of living waters, and hewed out cisterns for themselves, broken cisterns that can hold no water." (Jeremiah 2:11–13)

The heavens are appalled and shocked when people give up soon on their quest for pleasure and settle for broken cisterns. — John Piper, *Desiring God* (Sisters, OR: Multnomah Publishers, 2003), 98.

6. John 4.10 – 13. What exactly does Jesus mean by "living water"?

Don't you need regular sips from God's reservoir? I do. In countless situations— stressful meetings, dull days, long drives, demanding trips—and many times a day, I step to the underground spring of God. There I receive anew his work for my sin and death, the energy of his Spirit, his lordship, and his love.

Drink with me from his bottomless **well**. You don't have to live with a dehydrated heart.

Receive Christ's

Work on the cross, the

energy of his Spirit, his

Lordship over your life, his unending, unfailing

Love.

Drink deeply and often. And out of you will flow rivers of living water. — *Come Thirsty* / Max Lucado, *Grace for the Moment® Volume Ii: More Inspirational Thoughts for Each Day of the Year* (Nashville: Thomas Nelson, 2006).

7. **How is this life different than trying hard to be good?**

Jesus made shocking promises about his ability to transform human lives:

" 'Let anyone who is thirsty come to me and drink. Whoever believes in me, as Scripture has said, rivers of living water will flow from within them.' By this he meant the Spirit, whom those who believed in him were later to receive."

The King James Bible states it this way: "Out of his belly shall flow rivers of living water." The belly is the deepest place inside you—the place where you get anxious or afraid, where you feel hollow or empty when you're disappointed. It's in that very deepest place that Jesus says he'll produce vitality.

This life isn't something we produce; it exists without our help. It comes from the Spirit of God. — John Ortberg and Scott Rubin, *The Me I Want to Be, Teen Edition: Becoming God's Best Version of You* (Grand Rapids, MI: Zondervan, 2010).

8. **Can you think of other ways this life is described in the Bible?**

If we turn to any book in the New Testament, we see a picture of amazing life offered by Jesus through the Spirit.

"You will receive power when the Holy Spirit comes on you."

"Though you have not seen [Jesus], you love him...and are filled with an inexpressible and glorious joy."

"Take my yoke upon you and learn from me, for I am gentle and humble in heart, and you will find rest for your souls."

Would you say these verses describe you? Are you filled with glorious joy? Do others comment that you've pretty much aced the gentleness thing?

After people say yes to Jesus in their lives, there's usually a kind of spiritual honeymoon period. New Christians are filled with love for God, and they're drawn to the Bible. They want to tell other people about their faith. They love to worship. And some things change in their lives, too. Maybe foul language gets cleaned up. Maybe certain habits get overcome. — John Ortberg and Scott Rubin, *The Me I Want to Be, Teen Edition: Becoming*

God's Best Version of You (Grand Rapids, MI: Zondervan, 2010).

9. **What do Christians tend to do when we can't find a way to lay hold of this living water life?**

But after a little while, this sense of progress often stalls out. Instead of life flowing with rivers of living water, I yell at my family members. I worry too much about school or relationships. I get jealous. I lie to get out of trouble or to get what I want. I judge people easily and look down on them. My prayer life is on and off. I'm stuck in a gap.

God's plan is for you to become the best version of you, but right now there are two versions of you: The you God made you to be—and the you right now.

What do you do with the gap?

Gap Management

Our problem is that we believe we have to close the gap through our own **cleverness**. Some believe that if they just try harder, they can close the gap between the me God made them to be and the me right now. They believe they're just not being heroic enough in their spiritual efforts: "I'll work harder. I'll try to be nicer to the people in my life. I'll pray more. I'll pay more attention at youth group."

You hear about someone who gets up early in the morning to pray, and you feel guilty because you think you don't pray enough. So you make up your mind to wake up early, too (even though you're not a "morning person"). Only, when you wake up early, you're dazed and groggy and grumpy, and no one wants to be around you. You think, Well, this is exhausting and miserable. I sure don't like doing it—therefore, it must be God's will for my life. You keep it up for several days or weeks or maybe even months—but not forever. Eventually you stop. Then you feel guilty. After enough guilt, you start doing something else.

Sometimes we manage the gap by **pretending**. We learn to fake it. We speak as if we're walking closer to God than we really are, as though our sin bothers us more than it really does. We try to pray impressive prayers. Some people rush from one spiritual experience to another, continually rededicating their lives to God at camps or retreats or church services, hoping to recapture the emotions they felt when they first met God. And then they fall away again. — John Ortberg and Scott Rubin, *The Me I Want to Be, Teen Edition: Becoming God's Best Version of You* (Grand Rapids, MI: Zondervan, 2010).

10. What should we do to lay hold of this living water life?

Now the gap is between the me I am right now and the me I'm meant to be—"the now me" and "God's version of me." But here's the problem: A lot of us believe it's our job to bridge that gap. But we can't make that happen, either. This gap can be bridged only by grace. Improving yourself on your own makes as much sense as saving yourself on your own—you can't! God's plan isn't just for us to be saved by grace—it's for us to live by grace. God's plan is for my daily life to be given, guided, guarded, and energized by the grace of God. To live in grace is to flow in the Spirit.

We've now come to the most basic idea of this book (if you don't get anything else from reading these pages, please get this!): The only way to become the person God made you to be is to live with the Spirit of God flowing through you like a river of living water. The rest of this chapter will give a clear picture of what it looks like to live from one moment to the next in flow with the Spirit—not in following rules or trying harder—so you'll receive the power to Really Live as the me god made you to be. — John Ortberg and Scott Rubin, *The Me I Want to Be, Teen Edition: Becoming God's Best Version of You* (Grand Rapids, MI: Zondervan, 2010).

11. Ecclesiastes 3.11 says we have eternity in our hearts. What exactly does that mean?

We pilgrims walk the tightrope between earth and heaven, feeling trapped in time, yet with eternity beating in our hearts. Our unsatisfied sense of exile is not to be solved or fixed while here on earth. Our pain and longings make sure we will never be content, and that's good; it is to our benefit that we do not grow comfortable in a world destined for decay.

Joni Eareckson Tada, *Heaven: Your Real Home* — Randy Alcorn*, Eternal Perspectives: A Collection of Quotations on Heaven, the New Earth, and Life after Death* (Carol Stream, IL: Tyndale House Publishers, Inc., 2012).

12. Does this suggest that following God satisfies our thirst or makes us thirstier?

Homesickness—this perpetual experience of missing something—usually gets misdiagnosed and so wrongly treated. . . . All our lives we take hold of the wrong thing, go to the wrong place, eat the wrong food. We drink too much, sleep too much, work too long, take too many vacations or too few—all in the faint hope that this will finally satisfy us and so silence the hunger within.

. . . Here is the surprise: God made us this way. He made us to yearn—to always be hungry for something we can't get, to always be missing something we can't find, to always be disappointed with what we receive, to always have an insatiable emptiness that no thing can fill and an untamable restlessness that no discovery can still. Yearning itself is healthy—a kind of compass inside us, pointing to True North.

It's not the wanting that corrupts us. What corrupts us is the wanting that's misplaced, set on the wrong thing. If we don't understand that—if we don't understand that God has set eternity in our hearts to make us heavenly-minded, we skew or subvert the yearning and scatter it in a thousand wrong directions.

But the cure for our yearning and our restlessness is not to keep getting more. . . . The cure is to yearn for the right thing, the Unseen Things.

. . . We are metaphysically handicapped. This is not so much a design flaw as a designed flaw, a glitch wired into the system, a planned obsolescence.

. . . This shaking, unslaked desire in me is a divining rod for streams of Living Water. . . . He put in me, in you, a homing device for heaven. We just won't settle for anything less.50 — Mark Buchanan, *Things Unseen* — Randy Alcorn, *Eternal Perspectives: A Collection of Quotations on Heaven, the New Earth, and Life after Death* (Carol Stream, IL: Tyndale House Publishers, Inc., 2012).

13. Look over Psalm 139 silently. What do we learn about ourselves from this passage?

Do you understand how valuable you are? Cherished. Loved without limits. Wanted. At this moment, you may feel abandoned, or forsaken, or betrayed, but feelings are not trustworthy and can change at the drop of a rogue hormone. Now is the time to overrule your heart with your head. Re-read that scripture above. See how intimately your Papa God knows and adores you? You've gotta love that last line! He's still with you even though He knows you better than anyone in the entire world: inside out, failures and successes, rotten habits, and weird quirks. He will never leave you. He's absolutely dedicated to you! — Debora M. Coty, *Too Blessed to Be Stressed: 3-Minute Devotions for Women* (Uhrichsville, OH: Barbour, 2016).

14. What do we learn about God?

Where can you go to learn what God is like? Psalm 139. And the first thing you learn about is God's **omniscience** (vv. 1-6). God is all-knowing. He knows everything about you. He searches, perceives, discerns, and is familiar with everything about you. Whether you're in your car, at work, at home, or in the mountains, you cannot hide. In fact, God knows your thoughts. Every thought that has flashed across the screen of your mind is known to God. What does that mean to you?

Verses 7-12 teach about God's **omnipresence**. The verses here reflect David's amazement that God's hand is everywhere to guide him and to hold him. The psalmist gives several illustrations of the extent to which God is everywhere. How can this truth make a difference in your daily life? Have you ever explored this truth about God with your partner?

God's **omnipotence** is expressed in verses 13-18. He is the source of creative power. God can search you out not only because He knows you and is everywhere, but because He made you. You were not merely a thought in someone's mind. God is the one who brought you into being. That means you are significant. No wonder David spends verses 17,18 praising God!

What is the significance of God's **omniscience**, **omnipresence**, and **omnipotence** in your life as a couple today? How can your awareness of these qualities make a difference as you confront your work, your fears, your struggles, and your past and present hurts? How can your individual lives and your marriage be different because of God's omniscience, omnipresence, and omnipotence? These three big, meaningful words are used to help us understand the God who created us, who loved us enough to send His Son for us, and who wants us to love and worship Him. What a wonderful God we serve! — H. Norman Wright, *Quiet Times for Couples* (Eugene, OR: Harvest House, 2011).

15. **Read for application. We always want to read the Bible for application. (Have I said that before?) What is the application from this Psalm?**

This phrase in verse 9 reminds me of the race between the United States and the Soviet Union to get into space during the Cold War. A report from the Kremlin surfaced after their first space flight saying that they had traveled into space but did not see God. The late pastor W. A. Criswell from First Baptist Church of Dallas gave this classic response: "If he had stepped out of that spacesuit, he would have seen God!" Dr. Criswell was right —God is there. He made the planets, along with every single star. His majestic presence encompasses every galaxy.

When we apply that truth personally, it also serves as a reminder that no matter where we find ourselves, including the most remote or insignificant island in the sea, God is there, awaiting our arrival. If we were to escape to that tiny spot, hoping to hide from the consequences of some crime we'd committed, God would be right there. If we dragged a guilty conscience with us when we left, we'd find a guilty conscience when we arrived. As this verse is applied, we realize why travel will never bring us peace if we're at odds with the living God. As verse 7 affirms, we can never escape from His Spirit. We can never get away from His presence. — Charles R. Swindoll, *Searching the Scriptures: Find the Nourishment Your Soul Needs* (Carol Stream, IL: Tyndale House Publishers, Inc., 2016).

16. Isaiah 43.4 picks up on this same theme. Question. Can we make too much of God's love for us?

You have significance simply because I love you. You are My beloved child. That is your identity. Don't measure your value in terms of how successful you are or what roles you play. You are valuable because I have declared you precious and honored. When life feels mundane and you are caught up in laundry, work, or cooking, it's easy to doubt your importance in My kingdom. Nothing could be further from the truth. When feelings of insignificance torment you, come and praise Me. As you worship Me, your identity becomes more firmly rooted in Me, rather than in who you know or what you do. Thank Me for the price I paid for you. You are worth everything to Me. When you praise Me, you are more able to let go of worries about your worth and efforts to try to prove yourself. Always remember that you are a royal priest or priestess with a divine calling in My kingdom. It doesn't get any better than that! (1 John 3:1; Isa. 43:4; Eph. 1:4; 1 Cor. 6:20; 1 Peter 2:9)

Focus your praise time on the truth that you have value and worth as God's beloved child. Praise God that He calls you precious and honored. Because of Jesus Christ, your significance is ensured for all eternity. Praise Him that you have a divine calling as a royal priest or priestess.

You are precious and honored in my sight, and ... I love you. (Isa. 43:4) — Becky Harling, *The 30-Day Praise Challenge* (Colorado Springs, CO: David C. Cook, 2013).

17. Psalm 100.4. The thing we are missing is an awareness of the presence of God. We miss what the old timers called the manifest presence of God. How do we enter into the presence of God?

How important it is for each of us to know the way into God's presence! How do we enter His gates? How do we come into His courts? The psalmist points out the way that God has ordained: We enter His gates with thanksgiving, His courts with praise. It is only as we come to God with thanksgiving and with praise that we have access into His presence.

The prophet Isaiah likens the presence of God among His people to a city, concerning which he says: "You will call your walls Salvation and your gates Praise" (Isaiah 60:18). The only way through those walls of Salvation is by the gates of Praise. Unless we learn to approach God with praise, we have no access into His presence.

Confronted with this requirement, we are sometimes tempted to look around us at our situation and ask: "But what do I have to thank God for? What do I have to praise Him for?" There may be nothing in our immediate circumstances that appears to give us cause to thank or praise God. It is just here that the psalmist comes to our help. He gives us three reasons to thank and praise that are not affected by our circumstances: first, the Lord is good; second, His love endures forever; third, His faithfulness continues through all generations. All three are eternal, unchanging facts. If we truly believe them, then we have no alternative but to praise God for them—continually! — Derek Prince, *Through the Psalms with Derek Prince* (Grand Rapids, MI: Chosen Books, 2002).

18. John 4.24. Why is God looking for worshipers who worship in both Sprit and Truth?

The Father is seeking people to worship Him in spirit and truth (John 4:23,24). David said, "You who fear the LORD, praise Him; all you descendants of Jacob, glorify Him, and stand in awe of Him, all you descendants of Israel" (Psalm 22:23). An act of worship is to ascribe to God His divine attributes. We praise God for who He is, and we do this for our sake. God doesn't need us to tell Him who He is, but we need to keep His divine attributes constantly before us.

The form of worship isn't important so long as your worship of God is prompted by the Holy Spirit and in accordance with the truth of God's Word. You are worshiping God when you sing hymns or when you play a praise tape in your car. You can worship God by shouting praises to Him in the forest or bowing in silence before Him in your bedroom at home. You are worshiping God when you "do your work heartily, as for the Lord rather than for men" (Colossians 3:23). You can worship God anywhere at anytime in the quietness of your heart. You can worship God formally or informally, but never irreverently.

Nothing dispels a cloud of despair over our lives like uninhibited praise and worship of the King. He is worthy of it, and we need to do it. Worship reminds us of who God is and who we are in relation to Him. Pride crumbles and humility flourishes in the heart of worship. Worship is like a spiritual greenhouse in which the fear of God and love of God blossom. And as delightful as personal worship is, corporate worship is even better!

Few commands are repeated more often in Scripture than "praise the Lord." Three of the shortest commands in the Bible should always be on the lips of those who continuously worship God: "Rejoice always; pray without ceasing; in everything give thanks; for this is God's will for you in Christ Jesus" (1 Thessalonians 5:16-18). The writer of Hebrews says, "Through Him [Jesus] then, let us continually offer up a sacrifice of praise to God, that is, the fruit of lips that give thanks to His name" (Hebrews 13:15). — Neil Anderson and Rich Miller, *Freedom from Fear: Overcoming Worry and Anxiety* (Eugene, OR: Harvest House, 1999).

19. **What do you want to remember and apply from today's study?**

20. **How can we support one another in prayer this week?**

Not God Enough, Lesson #6
Chapter #9: The God We Hate
Chapter 10: Scandalous
Good Questions Have Groups Talking
www.joshhunt.com

OPEN:

Opening question: What is one thing almost certain to make you mad?

DIG

1. **Psalm 7.11 - 13. What do we learn about God from this verse?**

   7:11–13 This is the message we must bring to a sinful world. God is angry with the wicked every day. His wrath abides on them (John 3:36). Every time they sin, they are storing up for themselves wrath that will be revealed on the Day of Judgment (Romans 2:5). Unless they are convinced that there is wrath to come, they will not flee to the One who can deliver them from the wrath to come (1 Thessalonians 1:10). — Ray Comfort, *The Evidence Bible: Irrefutable Evidence for the Thinking Mind*, Notes, ed. Kirk Cameron, The Way of the Master Evidence Bible (Orlando, FL: Bridge-Logos, 2003), 710.

2. **Lewis said, There is no doctrine which I would more willingly remove from Christianity than this, if it**

lay in my power." He was speaking of Hell. Greear applies this idea to the wrath of God which is, of course, related to the Doctrine of Hell. What about you... would you get rid of this aspect of God if you could?

Some will not be redeemed. There is no doctrine which I would more willingly remove from Christianity than this, if it lay in my power. But it has the full support of Scripture and, specially, of Our Lord's own words; it has always been held by Christendom; and it has the support of reason. If a game is played, it must be possible to lose it. If the happiness of a creature lies in self-surrender, no one can make that surrender but himself (though many can help him to make it) and he may refuse. I would pay any price to be able to say truthfully 'All will be saved.' But my reason retorts 'Without their will, or with it?' If I say 'Without their will' I at once perceive a contradiction; how can the supreme voluntary act of self-surrender be involuntary? If I say 'With their will,' my reason replies 'How if they will not give in?' — C. S. Lewis, *The Problem of Pain* (New York: HarperOne, 2001), 119–120.

3. **Greear says, "GOD'S WRATH IS AN EXPRESSION OF HIS GOODNESS." What does he mean by that?**

God's wrath is an expression of His goodness, provoked when we choose to disobey Him, deserved, and meant to motivate us to live holy lives. It involves natural consequences, can lead to blessings being withdrawn, and is never to be interfered with to get back at those who have hurt us.

What an incredible God we have that His wrath is never hateful or cruel but rather always right, good, and merited. The next time we experience painful natural consequences or the withdrawal of blessing, we need to be grateful that God expresses His anger in ways that can ultimately benefit us if we will turn away from what we are doing wrong.

Job 5:17 tells us, "Blessed is the one whom God corrects; so do not despise the discipline of the Almighty." When we drill down into a verse such as that one, we can grow in our respect for God's righteousness and understand that He loves us too much to ignore our unrighteousness. We can go from resenting God's discipline to seeing that it comes out of His love for us and is aimed at helping us grow. Studying verses such as this leads to healthy shifts in our views of God's righteous anger toward sin and helps raise the bar for how we live. — Chris Thurman, *The Lies We Believe about God: Knowing God for Who He Really Is* (Colorado Springs, CO: David C. Cook, 2017).

4. **Before we get any further… What is wrath? How would you define it?**

Wrath is defined as "the emotional response to perceived wrong and injustice," often translated as "anger," "indignation," "vexation," or "irritation." Both humans and God express wrath. But there is vast difference between the wrath of God and the wrath of man. God's wrath is holy and always justified; man's is never holy and rarely justified. — Got Questions Ministries, *Got Questions? Bible Questions Answered* (Bellingham, WA: Logos Bible Software, 2002–2013).

5. **At first blush, we might want to get rid of the wrath of God if we could. But, if we think about it more deeply, we find that there is something deeply satisfying about the wrath of God. What is that?**

Again, we must be careful to communicate that God does not delight in taking revenge on sinners. Cranfield points out that God's wrath is an expression of his goodness. Humans who are not angry at injustice, cruelty, and corruption cannot be thoroughly good persons. If God is holy, God cannot tolerate willful transgression, indifference to the moral law, or the abuse of others. God honors our freedom to make all the wrong choices, but we will pay the price for snubbing God's love and mercy. Expunging God's holy wrath from our faith drains God's loving grace of any meaning. People need to hear more than the soothing message that God cares about you and "will bless you real good." God will also judge. — David E. Garland, *Colossians and Philemon, The NIV Application Commentary* (Grand Rapids, MI: Zondervan Publishing House, 1998), 219.

6. God loves us, but He can't stand our sin. He loves us, but He can't stand being around us. What is the solution?

Many people think that God can just forgive our sins because He's loving. Nothing could be further from the truth. The cross speaks to us not only about our sin but about God's holiness.

We usually think of God's holiness as His infinite moral purity, but there's more to it than that. The basic meaning of the word holy is "separate," and when used of God it means, among other things, that He's eternally separate from any degree of sin. He does not sin Himself, and He cannot abide or condone sin in His moral creatures.

He's not like the proverbial indulgent grandfather who winks at or ignores a grandchild's mischievous disobedience. Instead, God's holiness responds to sin with immutable and eternal hatred. To put it plainly, God hates sin. The psalmist said, "The boastful shall not stand before your eyes; you hate all evildoers," and "God is a righteous judge, a God who expresses his wrath every day" (Psalm 5:5; 7:11, NIV). God always hates sin and inevitably expresses His wrath against it.

The cross expresses God's holiness in His determination to punish sin, even at the cost of His Son. And it expresses His love in sending His Son to bear the punishment we so justly deserved.

We cannot begin to understand the true significance of the cross unless we understand something of the holiness of God and the depth of our sin. And a continuing sense of the imperfection of our obedience, arising from the constant presence and remaining power of indwelling sin, drives us more and more as believers to an absolute dependence on the grace of God given to us through His Son, our Lord Jesus Christ.
— Jerry Bridges, *Holiness Day by Day: Transformational Thoughts for Your Spiritual Journey*, ed. Thomas Womack (Colorado Springs, CO: NavPress, 2008), 35.

7. Romans 5.6 – 10. What does God reveal about Himself in this passage?

Thirty years after the crime, he was finally apprehended, tried, and found guilty by a jury. The arrest and conviction shocked both family and community. His life had been pleasant enough, raising a family, working as a salesman, even participating in many civic activities.

Men and women who are separated from God are in a similar predicament. While they may enjoy reasonably happy and successful lives, they live at enmity with their Creator and Judge.

Paul noted, "For if when we were enemies we were reconciled to God through the death of His Son" (Rom.

5:10). Other passages refer to man's alienation from God and his position as an enemy of "the cross of Christ" (Phil. 3:18).

Yet the love of God stretches across the chasm of sin and offers a solution to the hostility. The only path to true peace is faith in Christ's death, burial, and resurrection. That decision alone gives a person peace with God, establishing an eternal relationship with Christ.

True peace—the kind that lasts forever, the kind that reconciles God and man—is yours through faith in Christ. Don't deceive yourself or others with false appearances. Trust Him today. — Charles F. Stanley, *Into His Presence* (Nashville, TN: Thomas Nelson Publishers, 2000), 194.

8. **Circle the word "reconciled" in this passage. What exactly does it mean that we are reconciled?**

Reconciliation is changing for the better a relationship between two or more persons. Theologically it refers to the change of relationship between God and man. We are naturally children of wrath (Eph. 2:3), and are at enmity with God (Eph. 2:11–15); but, "...we were reconciled to God through the death of His Son..." (Rom. 5:10). Because of the death of Jesus, the Christian's relationship with God is changed for the better. We are now able to have fellowship with Him (1 John 1:3) whereas before we could not. So, we are reconciled to Him (Rom. 5:10–11). The problem of sin that separates us from God (Isaiah 59:2) has been addressed and removed in the cross. It was accomplished by God in Christ (2 Cor. 5:18). — Galaxie Software, *10,000 Sermon Illustrations* (Biblical Studies Press, 2002).

Chapter #10: Scandalous

9. **Chapter Ten. The title is "Scandalous." What is that about?**

Years later I'd discover the glorious news that when I was at my worst, Jesus Christ willingly died for me. He's done the same for you too. **What's wild is He offered His bloody and beaten body as a sacrificial offering to lift up our faithless and sin-stained bodies, clothing our messy and messed-up lives with His stunning, scandalous love.**

It's nearly too much to stand when you've come to know Jesus firsthand. By His saving grace, sinners are welcomed into the arms of a fascinating and forgiving Savior. All these years later, sitting in His embrace, drinking in His love, receiving His forgiveness, being washed in His grace—these never go threadbare. I might run away with a tinge of temporary insanity for a few moments, but on my return I'm always set back aright—safe and sound, quieted and reassured.

Then I'm happy I returned home. — Tammie Head, *More: From Messes to Miracles* (Nashville: B&H, 2015).

10. **1 John 3.1 What do we learn about ourselves from this passage?**

In His human journey, Jesus experienced God in a way that no prophet of Israel had ever dreamed or dared. Jesus was indwelt by the Spirit of the Father and given a name for God that would scandalize both the theology and public opinion of Israel, the name that escaped the mouth of the Nazarene carpenter: Abba.

Jewish children used this intimate colloquial form of speech in addressing their fathers. As a term for divinity, however, it was unprecedented not only in Judaism but in any of the great world religions. Joachim Jeremias wrote, "Abba, as a way of addressing God, is ipsissima vox, an authentic original utterance of Jesus. We are confronted with something new and astounding. Herein lies the great novelty of the gospel."1 Jesus, the Beloved Son, does not hoard this experience for Himself. He invites and calls us to share the same intimate and liberating relationship.

Paul wrote, "For all who are led by the Spirit of God are children of God. For you did not receive a spirit of slavery to fall back into fear but you have received a spirit of adoption. When we cry, 'Abba,' it is that spirit bearing witness with our spirit that we are children of God" (Romans 8:14-16). John, "the disciple Jesus loved," exclaims, "Think of the love the Father has lavished on us, by letting us be called God's children; and that is what we are" (1 John 3:1).

The greatest gift I have ever received from Jesus Christ has been the Abba experience. My dignity as Abba's child is my most coherent sense of self. — Brennan Manning, *The Rabbi's Heartbeat* (Colorado Springs, CO: NavPress, 2014).

11. Is this how you see yourself—as the object of God's scandalous love?

Years ago, I related a story about a priest from Detroit named Edward Farrell who visited his uncle in Ireland on his eightieth birthday. On the great day, they got up before dawn and went walking in silence along the shores of Lake Killarney and stopped to watch the sunrise. After they stood, side by side staring at the rising sun, suddenly the uncle turned and went skipping down the road. He was radiant, beaming, smiling from ear to ear.

His nephew said, "Uncle Seamus, you really look happy."

"I am, lad."

"Want to tell me why?"

His eighty-year-old uncle replied, "Yes, you see, my Abba is very fond of me."

How would you respond if I asked you this question? Do you honestly believe God likes you, not just loves you because theologically God has to love you?

Jesus, for "in his body lives the fullness of divinity" (Colossians 2:9), singularly understands the tenderness and compassion of the Father's heart. Why did Jesus love sinners, ragamuffins and the rabble who knew nothing of the law? Because His Abba loved them. He did nothing on His own, but only what His Abba told Him. Through meal-sharing, preaching, teaching, and healing, Jesus acted out His understanding of the Father's indiscriminate love— a love that causes His sun to rise on bad men as well as good, and His rain to fall on honest and dishonest men alike (Matthew 5:45). — Brennan Manning, *The Rabbi's Heartbeat* (Colorado Springs, CO: NavPress, 2014).

12. The story of Jonah is one example of God's scandalous love. Who can summarize that story?

The word of the Lord comes to Jonah:

> Could you, would you go to preach?
> Could you, would you go to reach
> The people in Assyria?
> For you fit my criteria.

And Jonah says to the Lord:

I would not go there in a boat.
I would not go there in a float.
I would not go there in a gale.
I would not go there in a whale.
I do not like the people there.
If they all died, I would not care.
I will not go to that great town.
I'd rather choke. I'd rather drown.
I will not go by land or sea.
So stop this talk and let me be.

God says, "Go."
Jonah says, "No."
God says, "Blow."
Jonah says, "So?"
The captain says, "Bro."
Jonah says, "Throw."
The sailors say, "Whoa!"
So they tossed Jonah in and he sank very low,
But God had more places for Jonah to go.

John Ortberg, *All the Places to Go . . . How Will You Know? God Has Placed before You an Open Door. What Will You Do?* (Carol Stream, IL: Tyndale House Publishers, Inc., 2015).

13. Jonah was called to preach to the Ninevites. What were they like?

Nineveh was the capital of one of the cruelest, vilest, most powerful, and most idolatrous empires in the world. For example, writing of one of his conquests, Ashurnaṣirpal II (883–859) boasted, "I stormed the mountain peaks and took them. In the midst of the mighty mountain I slaughtered them; with their blood I dyed the mountain red like wool.... The heads of their warriors I cut off, and I formed them into a pillar over against their city; their young men and their maidens

I burned in the fire" (Luckenbill, Ancient Records of Assyria and Babylonia, 1:148). Regarding one captured leader, he wrote, "I flayed [him], his skin I spread upon the wall of the city ..." (ibid., 1:146). He also wrote of mutilating the bodies of live captives and stacking their corpses in piles.

Shalmaneser II (859–824) boasted of his cruelties after one of his campaigns: "A pyramid of heads I reared in front of his city. Their youths and their maidens I burnt up in the flames" (ibid., 1:213). Sennacherib (705–681) wrote of his enemies, "I cut their throats like lambs. I cut off their precious lives [as one cuts] a string. Like the many waters of a storm I made [the contents of] their gullets and entrails run down upon the wide earth.... Their hands I cut off" (ibid., 2:127).

Ashurbanipal (669–626) described his treatment of a captured leader in these words: "I pierced his chin with my keen hand dagger. Through his jaw ... I passed a rope, put a dog chain upon him and made him occupy ... a kennel" (ibid., 2:319). In his campaign against Egypt, Ashurbanipal also boasted that his officials hung Egyptian corpses "on stakes [and] stripped off their skins and covered the city wall(s) with them" (ibid., 2:295).

No wonder Nahum called Nineveh "the city of blood" (3:1), a city noted for its "cruelty"! (3:19) — Elliott E. Johnson, "Nahum," in *The Bible Knowledge Commentary: An Exposition of the Scriptures*, ed. J. F. Walvoord and R. B. Zuck, vol. 1 (Wheaton, IL: Victor Books, 1985), 1494.

14. What is the lesson for us?

God loved Nineveh. Idolatrous, unspeakably cruel, barbaric, Nineveh. That in itself is a sign that He loves and reaches out to you. God's pursuit of the Ninevites is proof that his grace stretches to you wherever you are. — J. D. Greear, "Something Greater than Jonah: Matthew 12:38–41," *in J. D. Greear Sermon Archive* (Durham, NC: The Summit Church, 2017), Mt 12:38–41.

15. Hosea is another example of God's scandalous love. Who can refresh our memories about that story?

In Hosea 1:2 we read, "The LORD said to Hosea, 'Go, take to yourself a wife of whoredom and have children of whoredom.' " Hosea obeyed, marrying a woman named Gomer, who was unfaithful to him. Why did God tell Hosea to marry a prostitute?

To begin with, it is important to realize this command could be understood two different ways. First, and more likely, this command could be one of anticipation. In other words, God may have instructed Hosea to marry a woman who would later become unfaithful to him. The other possibility is that the command was for Hosea to marry someone already known as a prostitute.

In either case, the reason for this unusual directive is specified in the latter half of the same verse: "For the land commits great whoredom by forsaking the LORD." God wanted to provide an illustration of His relationship with the people of Israel, who had been unfaithful to Him by practicing idolatry. This theme is carried through the remainder of the prophecies in chapter 1 and the discussion of Israel's unfaithfulness in chapter 2.

In Hosea 3:1, after Gomer had left Hosea and was living in immorality, the Lord commanded Hosea to find her and buy her back. God was continuing His illustration, except now He wanted to show the greatness of His grace: "Even as the LORD loves the children of Israel, though they turn to other gods." Hosea's faithful love of Gomer was an illustration of God's faithfulness to wayward Israel. Just as Gomer had been unfaithful to her husband and had to be redeemed, Israel needed God's initiative to restore their relationship.

The prophet Hosea was commanded to marry an unfaithful wife, and this set up a model of Israel's broken relationship with God. Israel had been chosen and loved by God yet had been unfaithful to Him by way of idolatry. Just as Hosea redeemed his estranged wife and sought to continue his relationship with her, God promised to redeem Israel and renew their relationship with Him. The story of Hosea and Gomer is an unforgettable picture of God's strong, unending love for His covenant people. — Got Questions Ministries, *Got Questions? Bible Questions Answered* (Bellingham, WA: Logos Bible Software, 2002–2013).

16. What is the message of Hosea for us?

This background lies behind the Lord's command to the prophet Hosea to marry a prostitute (Hosea 1:2). What a scandalous sign to the people of Israel of their unfaithfulness! — Anthony E. Bird, *Practice Makes Perfect: The Book of James Simply Explained, Welwyn Commentary Series* (Darlington, England: EP Books, 2009), 159.

17. One more: The Prodigal Father. We normally refer to this story as The Prodigal Son. Why does Greear call it The Prodigal Father?

This is precisely why the Lord has given us this remarkable tale in Luke 15—the story we commonly call the Parable of the Prodigal Son—because a story illustrating love in the most fundamental of relationships will readily be understood by all. The parable could be called "The Parable of the Prodigal God" because the word prodigal means "extremely generous or lavish," and the story is primarily about the lavishness of God's love—that it is "an incomprehensibly vast, bottomless, shoreless sea." But the parable also gives us a unique opportunity to take our own spiritual temperature by observing how we relate to God's extravagant love through the characters of the two brothers. Where we stand depends on how well we are able to step into the skin of first the younger brother, and then the older. — R. Kent Hughes, *Luke: That You May Know the Truth, Preaching the Word* (Wheaton, IL: Crossway Books, 1998), 140.

18. What does this story teach us about ourselves?

If God had a refrigerator, your picture would be on it. If he had a wallet, your photo would be in it. He sends you flowers every spring and a sunrise every morning. Whenever you want to talk, he'll listen. He can live anywhere in the universe, and he chose your heart....

Face it, friend. He's crazy about you. — Max Lucado and Terri A. Gibbs, *Grace for the Moment: Inspirational Thoughts for Each Day of the Year* (Nashville, TN: J. Countryman, 2000), 87.

19. Why is it important that we know and understand and savor God's love for us?

As true as it is that hurt people do in turn hurt other people, it is also true that loved people love other people. Oftentimes, our struggles in relationships happen because one or more of the persons involved believe that they are not truly loved. They can't move past their insecurity. We are "acceptance magnets" because we were created to be loved. You are designed to hear someone say "I love you" and mean it with all their heart.

We have listened to the lies of the enemy for far too long, thinking that our difficult experiences confirm the untruth he speaks. You're only worth what you can do, whispers the enemy. You deserve everything that's been done to you. You deserve to struggle today. — Shelley Hendrix, *Why Can't We Just Get along? 6 Effective Skills for Dealing with Difficult People* (Eugene, OR: Harvest House, 2013).

20. What do you want to remember and apply from today's study?

21. How can we pray for each other this week?

Not God Enough, Lesson #7
Chapter #11: How to Confuse an Angel
Chapter #12: Catching Fire
Good Questions Have Groups Talking
www.joshhunt.com

OPEN:

Opening question: what is one favorite worship song?

DIG

1. 1 Peter 1.10 – 12. What amazes the angels?

After Peter warms our hearts in 1 Peter 1 with a description of our salvation, he adds, "Even angels long to look into these things" (1:12). What exactly are "these things"? Don't angels already understand the details of our salvation better than we do? Surely they have a better vantage point than we do down here.

Peter's words are a good reminder that what counts in the Christian life is personal experience, not head knowledge. Yes, angels certainly have intellectual awareness — "head knowledge" — of our salvation. But they haven't felt salvation or feasted on it. Therefore they "long to look into these things" because they understand that personal acquaintance is far better than mental comprehension. They have no pride about what they merely know; they long instead for experience.

— David Jeremiah, *What the Bible Says about Angels: Powerful Guardians, a Mysterious Presence, God's Messengers* (Sisters, OR: Multnomah Books, 1996), 108.

2. What else does the Bible teach about angels?

Angels are persons—spirit persons (Hebrews 1:14)—with all the attributes of personality: mind, emotions, and will. We know angels have minds because they have great wisdom (2 Samuel 14:20), exercise great discernment (2 Samuel 14:17), and use their minds to look into matters (1 Peter 1:12).

We know the angels have emotions because they gather in "joyful assembly" in the presence of God in heaven (Hebrews 12:22 NIV), "shouted for joy" at the creation (Job 38:7), and rejoice in heaven whenever a sinner repents (Luke 15:7).

Angels certainly give evidence of having a moral will in the many moral decisions they make. For example, an angel exercised his moral will in forbidding John to worship him, acknowledging that worship belongs only to God (Revelation 22:8-9).

In addition to having the basic attributes of personality, angels also engage in personal actions. For example, angels love and rejoice (Luke 15:10), they express desire (1 Peter 1:12), they contend (Jude 9; Revelation 12:7), they engage in worship (Hebrews 1:6), they talk (Luke 1:13), and they come and go (Luke 9:26). Angels also have personal names, such as Michael and Gabriel. Clearly, angels are every bit as much persons as human beings are. — Ron Rhodes, *5-Minute Apologetics for Today: 365 Quick Answers to Key Questions* (Eugene, OR: Harvest House, 2010).

3. Mark 14.33 – 34. What is Jesus feeling in this in this part of the story?

The strong statement of his amazement opens before us a curious problem. His fate, as he comes to face it, is not only troubling, but amazing. His rejection by men, their fierce hatred of him, his isolation of spirit, even among his own—all these things coming to the Son of Man, the lover of his kind, whose whole life was wrought by love into the fibre and tissue of the common human life, and was individual in no sense—amazed him utterly. περίλυπος—encompassed by grief. ἕως θανάτου—unto death. My sorrow is killing me, is the thought; it is crushing the life out of me. — Ezra Palmer Gould, *A Critical and Exegetical Commentary on the Gospel according to St. Mark, International Critical Commentary* (New York: C. Scribner's Sons, 1922), 269.

4. Why is Jesus so stressed?

Pull yourself together!" We struggle with our emotions so often! It's important to remember that our Savior experienced strong emotions throughout His earthly life, too.

The night before His crucifixion, Jesus cried out in prayer, asking for the "cup"—the crucifixion and separation from the Father—to pass from Him if possible. While Jesus was asking for another way, He also surrendered Himself to the Father—"Yet not what I will, but what you will" (Mark 14:36 NIV). Jesus remained sinless in His obedience to God even while He felt so overwhelmed that He could die from sorrow.

Jesus shows us that even the most heartrending emotions aren't sinful in themselves. It is possible to feel intense emotion but continue to trust God and act obediently (Psalm 4:4-5). Bring those feelings to

Jesus freely, because He understands what it's like. In your hardest times, He won't sigh and tell you to "get it together." He invites you instead to come to Him with your burdens so He can help you carry them (1 Peter 5:7). — Renae Brumbaugh et al., *One-a Daily Devotional: One Way, One Truth, One Life* (Uhrichsville, OH: Barbour, 2015).

5. What do we learn about fear from this example? What is the lesson for us?

WHAT DO YOU FEAR? Boarding an airplane? Facing a crowd?

Public speaking? Taking a job? Taking a spouse? Driving on a highway? The source of your fear may seem small to others. But to you, it freezes your feet, makes your heart pound, and brings blood to your face. That's what happened to Jesus.

Jesus was more than anxious; he was afraid. . . . How remarkable that Jesus felt such fear. But how kind that he told us about it. We tend to do the opposite. Gloss over our fears. Cover them up. Keep our sweaty palms in our pockets, our nausea and dry mouths a secret. Not so with Jesus. We see no mask of strength. But we do hear a request for strength.

"Father, if you are willing, take away this cup of suffering." The first one to hear his fear is his Father. He could have gone to his mother. He could have confided in his disciples. He could have assembled a prayer meeting. All would have been appropriate, but none were his priority. He went first to his father. — Max Lucado, *Traveling Light Journal* (Nashville: Thomas Nelson, 2001).

6. Hebrews 12.1 – 2. What motivated Jesus to go through with the cross?

Jesus was motivated by joy. Listen to Hebrews chapter 12, verse 2. The Bible says we are to be "looking unto Jesus, the author and finisher of our faith, who for the joy that was set before him endued the cross, despising the shame." What was the joy that was set before Him? You! What did the apostle Paul say about those people that he had led to Christ? He said in 1 Thessalonians chapter 2, verse 19: "For what is our hope, our joy, or our crown of rejoicing? Are not even ye in the presence of our Lord Jesus Christ at his coming?" — Adrian Rogers, "Every Christian's Job," in *Adrian Rogers Sermon Archive* (Signal Hill, CA: Rogers Family Trust, 2017), Jn 20:21.

7. What exactly was the joy set before Him?

The joy set before him had many levels. It was the joy of reunion with his Father: "In your presence there is fullness of joy; at your right hand are pleasures forevermore" (Psalm 16:11). It was the joy of triumph over sin: "After making purification for sins, he sat down at the right hand of the Majesty on high" (Hebrews 1:3). It was the joy of divine rights restored: "[He] is seated at the right hand of the throne of God" (Hebrews 12:2). It was the joy of being surrounded with praise by all the people for whom he died: "There will be … joy in heaven over one sinner who repents"—not to mention millions (Luke 15:7).

Now what about us? Has he entered into joy and left us for misery? No. Before he died, he made the connection between his joy and ours. He said, "These things I have spoken to you, that my joy may be in you, and that your joy may be full" (John 15:11). He knew what his joy would be, and he said, "My joy will be in you." We who have trusted in him will rejoice with as much of the joy of Jesus as finite creatures can experience. — John Piper, *Fifty Reasons Why Jesus Came to Die* (Wheaton, IL: Crossway Books, 2006), 114–115.

8. What do we learn about ourselves from this passage?

Jesus looked forward to the joy of spending eternity with you and me so much that He couldn't stand the thought of missing out on that. For the joy set before Him—His own joy—He stayed on the cross. Looking forward to the coming joy He would experience motivated Him to endure the cross. It is an amazing thing that Jesus was motivated by the joy of spending eternity with you and me. Athletes motivate themselves the same way, although, to a much lesser degree. Athletes like to say, "No pain; no gain." They see the joy before them that motivates them to endure the pain.

Jesus died because He loves us. John 3:16 is perhaps the most famous sentence in any language. God loves the world so much that He sent His one and only Son to die. Very rarely would someone die for someone else. (Romans 5:7) It is an expression of ultimate love. There are very few people I would die for. You only die for people you really, really love. (Romans 5:8) God really, really loves you, and Jesus' death is an expression of that love. — Josh Hunt, *The Habit of Discipleship* (Pulpit Press, 2015).

9. For the joy of spending time with us Jesus endured the cross. How does that affect us today?

Remember that your love relationship with God is alive and active. It must be cultivated on a daily basis. You'll have to keep sowing the seeds of this love—and the more you sow, the more you'll grow.

As long as there are life and breath in your body, you have the call from Christ to keep growing—to grow deeper, richer, and fuller in God's love. Your growth will come from staying connected to God and His word. Before you can ever be effective in serving God publicly, you must practice His presence by serving Him privately. This is the mark of true maturity.

Keep walking in the love that God has for you. Some days you'll be tired. Other days you'll be disappointed or discouraged. On days like these, you'll just need to keep putting one foot in front of the other. See yourself as God sees you:

- loved beyond your capacity to imagine;

- saved from your sins;

- healed from all diseases;

- delivered from the bondages of sin;

- free to live the life God has planned for you.

Keep reminding yourself over and over again of who and whose you are. This exercise will impact the way you think and ultimately the way you live.

No matter what tomorrow may bring, remember that God loves you and there is no need to fear the future because God is already there. He will give you just what you need, exactly the way you need it, at the precise moment you need it. God loves you as if you were the only one to love. You are His favorite. May this truth forever rock your world. And as you live loved day by day, returning the loving embrace of the Father, may you never, ever be the same! — Babbie Mason, *Seven Promises for Every Woman: From Embraced by God Women's Bible Study* (Nashville: Abingdon Press, 2012).

10. Ephesians 1:17–18; 3:16–19. What was Paul's prayer for the Ephesians?

Paul prays that the readers of his Ephesian letter "may have power, together with all the saints, to grasp how wide and long and high and deep is the love of Christ, and to know this love that surpasses knowledge" (Eph 3:18-19). The touch of incoherence and paradox in his language reflects Paul's sense that the reality of divine love is inexpressibly great; nevertheless, he believes that some comprehension of it can be reached. How?

The answer of Ephesians is, by considering propitiation in its context—that is, by reviewing the whole plan of grace set forth in the first two chapters of the letter (election, redemption, regeneration, preservation, glorification), of which plan the atoning sacrifice of Christ is the centerpiece. See the key references to redemption and "remission of sins" and the bringing near to God of those who were far off, through the blood (sacrificial death) of Christ (1:7; 2:13). See also the teaching of chapter 5, which twice points to Christ's propitiatory sacrifice of himself on our behalf as the demonstration and measure of his love for us, the love that we are to imitate in our dealings with each other. "Live a life of love, just as Christ loved us and gave himself up for us as a fragrant offering and sacrifice to God" (5:2). "Husbands, love your wives, just as Christ loved the church and gave himself up for her" (5:25).

Christ's love was free, not elicited by any goodness in us (2:15); it was eternal, being one with the choice of sinners to save which the Father made "before the creation of the world" (1:4); it was unreserved, for it led him down to the depths of humiliation and, indeed, of hell itself on Calvary; and it was sovereign, for it has achieved its object—the final glory of the redeemed, their perfect holiness and happiness in the fruition of his love (5:26-27), is now guaranteed and assured (1:14; 2:7-10; 4:11-16; 4:30). Dwell on these things, Paul urges, if you would catch a sight, however dim, of the greatness and the glory of divine love. It is these things that make up "his glorious grace (1:6); only those who know them can praise the name of the triune Jehovah as they should. Which brings us to our last point. — J.I. Packer, *Knowing God,* 1973.

Chapter #12: Catching Fire

11. How is a helium balloon a picture of Spirit-filled Christian living?

Discipleship is about living in the flow of the Spirit. It is about the Holy Spirit living His life through us. It is not about trying really hard to be good. If you are living a life of trying really hard to be good, I know one thing: you are tired. — Josh Hunt, *The Habit of Discipleship* (Pulpit Press, 2015).

12. 2 Corinthians 3.18. What do we learn about Christian living from this verse?

Transformed by beholding

Romans 12:2 is the most iconic and perhaps important verse on how we are transformed. Transformed by the renewing of our mind. Never forget that. But, it is not the only thing the Bible says about how we are transformed. This verse is equally important:

> And we all, with unveiled face, beholding the glory of the Lord, are being transformed into the same image from one degree of glory to another. 2 Corinthians 3:18a (ESV)

We become what we behold. We wind up like what we worship. We advance toward what we adore.

It is true in many arenas in life. Again, an example from tennis. Research shows that people who watch great tennis players become better. This is especially true if they imagine themselves moving like the pros.

> Many amateurs report that seeing tennis played at the highest level improves their own games.

> Watching tennis and playing it can be mutually helpful activities, dialectically entwined.

Jon Levey, a writer and avid player said: "I always play better after watching the pros. Their form shows you that less is more. They move their body weight into the ball much better than I do. Everything seems to work in symmetry. After the Open, I suddenly know how to hit 'up' on my serve, like they do.

This is part of what makes idolatry so dangerous. Not only is it a slap in God's face, it is damaging to us. Idolatry hurts the idolater.

What people revere, they resemble, either for ruin or restoration.

God has made humans to reflect him, but if they do not commit themselves to him, they will not reflect him but something else in creation. At the core of our beings we are imaging creatures. It is not possible to be neutral on this issue: we either reflect the Creator or something in creation. — Josh Hunt, *How to Live the Christian Life*, 2016.

13. How does worship change the worshiper?

What is discipleship, anyway? There could be a number of answers to this question, but central to what it means is that Jesus becomes Lord of my life in daily practice. James Smith defines it this way:

> In short, if you are what you love, and love is a habit, then discipleship is a rehabituation of your loves. This means that discipleship is more a matter of reformation than of acquiring information. The learning that is fundamental to Christian formation is affective and erotic, a matter of "aiming" our loves, of orienting our desires to God and what God desires for his creation.

When I worship, this process is almost automatic. When I sing, "He is Lord!" He becomes Lord in my daily decisions. I come to realize He is God and I am not; He is boss, I am slave; He is King, I am servant. Hours and hours of complicated Greek Bible studies won't get that in your head and heart like a good hour of worship. — Josh Hunt, *How to Live the Christian Life,* 2016.

14. Perhaps someone is thinking, "But, I don't like worship all that much." What would you say to them?

A church I was a member of at one stage in life did a night of worship once in a while. We called it T.G.O.F. — Thank God on Friday. The service consisted of about two and a half hours of uninterrupted worship. Uninterrupted, with the exception of an intermission about half-way through. (The heart cannot absorb what the seat cannot endure.)

It was glorious. I was telling a friend once that I thought that is what Heaven will be like—unending adoration of our glorious God. Hands lifted. Voice raised. We will all be able to sing like Chris Tomlin. We will sing loud. We will jump and shout and dance in the presence of the Lord. Even Baptists will dance. Wow. Hour after hour, day after day. My friend surprised me with his response. "I think that sounds awful." It was at that moment that I began to wonder if he were the Christian he professed to be.

Another odd thought occurred to me. If God were to allow everyone into Heaven, it would only be heavenly for those whose hearts have been changed. For my friend, Heaven would be Hell for him, by his own admission. It occurs to me that Heaven and Hell could be the same place—the place of manifest, inescapable, palpable presence of God. For those who have come to love God, having Him so real we can touch Him will be Heaven. For those who spend their life running from God, there will be no place to run. No place to hide. They can't get away. It will be hell.

Worship gets it clear in my head and heart who is Boss. — Josh Hunt, *How to Live the Christian Life*, 2016.

15. Revelation 4.2. What do we learn about God from this verse?

Worship reminds me that our Big God has it all in control

One of my favorite verses is Revelation 4:2:

> At once I was in the Spirit, and there before me was a throne in heaven with someone sitting on it. Revelation 4:2 (NIV2011)

Sitting.

Not pacing. Not surprised. Not wringing His hands. Not wondering. Not worrying. Large and in charge.

From my worms-eye view, it sometimes looks like the world is running recklessly out of control. It is not. There is a throne in Heaven. Someone is sitting.

It is impossible for me to worship and worry. You don't overcome worry by trying really hard not to worry. You overcome worry by worship. If you have a big God, you have small problems and you worry little. If you have a small God, you have big problems and you worry much. Nothing gets that straight like worship. — Josh Hunt, *How to Live the Christian Life,* 2016.

16. Is worship an advanced curriculum for the super-spiritual, or is it a core curriculum for all Christians?

Worship is not optional. In Matthew 4:10, in response to Satan's temptation, Jesus quoted Deuteronomy 6:13: "You shall worship the Lord your God, and serve Him only." In saying that to Satan, He swept into the command every being ever created. All are responsible to worship God.

The foundation upon which true worship is based is redemption. The Father and Son have sought to redeem us that we may become worshipers. Jesus said that the Son of Man came into the world to seek and to save that which was lost (Luke 19:10). In John 4 He reveals the purpose for His seeking: "For such people the Father seeks to be His worshipers" (v. 23). The Father sent Christ to seek and save for the specific purpose of producing worshiping people.

Thus, the objective of redemption is making worshipers. The primary reason we are redeemed is not so that we may escape hell—that is a blessed benefit, but not the major purpose. The central objective for which we are redeemed is not even so that we might enjoy the manifold eternal blessings of God. In fact, the supreme motive in our redemption is not for us to receive anything. Rather, we have been redeemed so that God may receive worship—so that our lives might glorify Him. Any personal blessing for us is a divine response to the fulfillment of that supreme purpose.

Paul affirmed that when he described his purpose of evangelism in Romans 1:5: "[We preach] obedience of faith among all the Gentiles for His name's sake" (emphasis added). John echoes that in 3 John 7. He writes that missionaries were sent out to proclaim the gospel "for the sake of the Name." Our salvation is first of all for God's benefit. — John MacArthur Jr., *The Ultimate Priority: John MacArthur, Jr. on Worship*, electronic ed. (Chicago: Moody Press, 1998), 23–24.

17. What are some practical ways we can make worship a part of our daily lives?

Chris Tomlin often leads me in worship during my morning Quiet Time. And, when Chris Tomlin is leading, it is normally glorious. There are a number of ways to get Chris Tomlin on your TV, including:

- A Smart TV

- Roku Box

- Amazon Fire TV

- Apple TV

- Chromecast

Pretty much anything that can get the Internet onto your TV will work. Do a search for "Chris Tomlin live worship" within the YouTube app and Voilà! Chris Tomlin leads you in worship. What a time to be alive! — Josh Hunt, *How to Live the Christian Life*, 2016.

18. We often think of worship as singing or listening to music—which is a good thing. How else can we worship?

There are a number of ways to worship:

- Psalms. Many of the Psalms were designed for worship. Read them and adore God. Read them and change. Read them and be transformed.

- Attributes of God. Meditate on the bigness of God, the goodness of God, the everywhereness of God. Think about the idea that God knows everything. If you put a nail through this book He would know what word and what letter the nail touched on every page. He could tell you the etymology of every word. He could translate every word into any language.

- Names of God. El Shaddai (Lord God Almighty); El Elyon (The Most High God); Adonai (Lord, Master); Yahweh (Lord, Jehovah); Jehovah Nissi (The Lord My Banner); Jehovah-Raah (The Lord My Shepherd); Jehovah Rapha (The Lord That Heals); Jehovah Shammah (The Lord Is There); Jehovah Tsidkenu (The Lord Our Righteousness); Jehovah Mekoddishkem (The Lord Who Sanctifies You); El Olam (The Everlasting God); Elohim (God); Qanna (Jealous); Jehovah Jireh (The Lord Will Provide); Jehovah Shalom (The Lord Is Peace); Jehovah Sabaoth (The Lord of Hosts)

- Nature. I can't prove it, but I believe Jacob was looking at a sunset in this verse: "By faith Jacob, when he was dying, blessed each of Joseph's sons, and worshiped as he leaned on the top of his staff." Hebrews 11:21 (NIV2011) I picture Jacob looking out at a sunset and thinking about the bigness and beauty of God. I nearly always do that when I look at a sunset. I can't help myself.

- Music. More than all of the above, nothing tunes my heart to worship like music.

Josh Hunt, *How to Live the Christian Life*, 2016.

19. What is one simple and specific thing you could do to apply today's lesson?

20. How can we pray for each other this week?

Not God Enough, Lesson #8
Chapter #13: It Is Not About You
Good Questions Have Groups Talking
www.joshhunt.com

OPEN:

Opening question: When was the last time you looked—really looked—at the stars?

DIG

1. **The Copernicus Revolution is a picture of what happens to us as we grow in discipleship. How so?**

   In the sixteenth century, the Renaissance astronomer Nicholas Copernicus challenged the belief that the earth was the center of the universe. Copernicus argued that the sun didn't revolve around the earth, but rather that the earth revolved around the sun. The Copernican Revolution turned the scientific world upside down by turning the universe inside out.

   In much the same way, each one of us needs to experience our own Copernican Revolution. The paradigm shift happens when we come to terms with the fact that the world doesn't revolve around us. But that's a tough pill to swallow.

   When we are born into this world, the world revolves around us. We're spoonfed on the front end and diaper-changed on the back end. It's as if the entire world exists to meet our every need. And that's fine if you are a two-month-old baby. If you're twenty-two, it's a problem!

Newsflash: You are not the center of the universe! — Mark Batterson, *Going All in: One Decision Can Change Everything* (Grand Rapids, MI: Zondervan, 2013).

2. How is life different—and better—after our own personal Copernican Revolution?

"All I Really Need to Know I Learned in Kindergarten," says Robert Fulgham's popular essay and book. In truth, one of life's most important and hardest lessons comes to us long before kindergarten. This lesson is painful and upsetting to learn, and it goes against what we want to think is true. But it is vital that we learn it. Many people never do. The lesson is this: you are not the center of your universe. You might as well face it. Once, a long time ago, Nicolaus Copernicus studied the sky and declared, "If man is to know the truth, he must change his thinking! Despite what we have said for years, our earth is not the center of the cosmos—but just one celestial body among many. The sun does not move around us; we move around the sun." That was a radical adjustment—a revolution in thought. Years later, Jean Piaget studied children and declared, "Each child must experience his or her own 'Copernican revolution.' They must learn that they are not the center of their world." This is a private, radical adjustment for every one. "After all," each infant thinks, "My wants have always been met. Let life continue that way!" "Walls should move out of the way before I run into them. The floor should become soft just as I fall. Everyone should give me their toys if I want them. The rules of games should change so I can always win. And big things like cars should never drive where I might want to run or play." Sooner or later, life does not cooperate and the child is shocked. What about us adults? Have we learned the lesson? Most of us learn it. But Satan urges us to put ourselves back in the center. And we often do, even when we know better. Jesus Christ studied His audience and declared, "If you want to enter the kingdom of heaven, you must change your thinking! Despite what your sinful nature tells you, you are not the center of your world. To find life, you must know the truth. Accommodate yourself to that; it will set you free!" That is the most radical adjustment of all. A hard lesson. The illusion is easier. It justifies selfishness. And we all like being selfish. Too bad that the selfish way is not true. Too bad that it does not bring satisfaction or life. A hard lesson. But an important one. Life goes much better once you have got it. — AMG Bible Illustrations, *Bible Illustrations Series* (Chattanooga: AMG Publishers, 2000).

3. **We are going to get to the Bible in just a second, but two more questions first. Greear mentions John Piper's book *Desiring God*. Has anyone read this book? What is the main message of this book?**

God is most glorified in me when I am most satisfied in Him. — John Piper, *Desiring God* (Sisters, OR: Multnomah Publishers, 2003), 10.

4. **This book has actually been a bit controversial. How so?**

The ultimate ground of Christian Hedonism is the fact that God is uppermost in His own affections:

The chief end of God is to glorify God and enjoy Himself forever.

The reason this may sound strange is that we are more accustomed to think about our duty than God's design.

And when we do ask about God's design, we are too prone to describe it with ourselves at the center of God's affections. We may say, for example, that His design is to redeem the world. Or to save sinners. Or to restore creation. Or the like.

But God's saving designs are penultimate, not ultimate. Redemption, salvation, and restoration are not God's ultimate goal. These He performs for the sake of something greater: namely, the enjoyment He has in glorifying Himself. The bedrock foundation of Christian Hedonism is not God's allegiance to us, but to Himself.

If God were not infinitely devoted to the preservation, display, and enjoyment of His own glory, we could have no hope of finding happiness in Him. But if He does in fact employ all His sovereign power and infinite wisdom to maximize the enjoyment of His own glory, then we have a foundation on which to stand and rejoice.

I know this is perplexing at first glance. So I will try to take it apart a piece at a time, and then put it back together at the end of the chapter. — John Piper, *Desiring God* (Sisters, OR: Multnomah Publishers, 2003), 31–32.

5. **Psalm 19:1; 1 Corinthians 10:31; Psalm 106:8; Isaiah 48:9; Isaiah 48:11; Ezekiel 36:22–23; Ephesians 1:4–6. What is the thread that ties all these verses together?**

The concept of worship dominates the Bible. In Genesis, we discover that the Fall came when man failed to worship God. In Revelation we learn that all of history culminates in an eternal worshiping community in the presence of a loving God. From the beginning in Genesis all the way through to the consummation in Revelation, the doctrine of worship is woven into the warp and woof of the biblical text.

Jesus quoted Deuteronomy 6:4–5 and called it the greatest commandment: "Hear, O Israel! The Lord our God is one Lord; and you shall love the Lord your God with all your heart, and with all your soul, and with all your mind, and with all your strength" (Mark 12:29–30). That is a call for worship, and it affirms worship as the universal priority.

Exodus 20 records the giving of the Ten Commandments. The very first of those commandments calls for and regulates worship:

> I am the Lord your God, who brought you out of the land of Egypt, out of the house of slavery. You shall have no other gods before Me. You shall not make for yourself an idol, or any likeness of what is in heaven above or on the earth beneath or in the water under the earth. You shall not worship them or serve them; for I, the Lord your God, am a jealous God. [vv. 2–5]

In the Old Testament, worship covered all of life; it was the focus of the people of God. For example, the Tabernacle was designed and laid out to emphasize the priority of worship. The description of its details requires seven chapters—243 verses—in Exodus, yet only 31 verses in Genesis are devoted to the creation of the world.

The Tabernacle was designed only for worship. It was the place where God met His people, and to use it for anything but worship would have been considered the grossest blasphemy. In the Tabernacle there were no seats—the Israelites didn't go there to attend a service, and they didn't go there for entertainment. They went there to worship God. If they had a meeting for any other purpose, they had it somewhere else. — John MacArthur Jr., *The Ultimate Priority: John MacArthur, Jr. on Worship,* electronic ed. (Chicago: Moody Press, 1998), 2–3.

6. Psalm 106.8. What motivates God?

I remember reading in a devotional book some years ago that the only thing that motivates God is His own glory. To our tiny minds that may sound egotistical, but we must remember that God is the Creator and the One to whom glory is due in the purity and beauty of His holiness. He deserves it.

I am motivated by so many lesser things, even in my prayer life: perhaps especially in my prayer life. God's glory should be our sole – and soul – motivation that frames and filters everything we pray. John Piper reiterated, "The chief end of man is to glorify God and enjoy Him forever. And the chief act of man by which the unity of these two goals is preserved is prayer."2

In John 14:13, Jesus gave us a standard for all of our praying, "And whatever you ask in My name, that I will do, that the Father may be glorified in the Son." What motivates us to ask can often be all over the map. What motivates our Father to answer is that He would be glorified in our prayers through the person and work of His Son, Jesus Christ. Jonathan Edwards, the great Puritan preacher and author, wrote, "It appears that all that is ever spoken of in the Scriptures as an ultimate end of God's works is included in that one phrase, 'the glory of God.' " — Daniel Henderson and Jim Cymbala, *Transforming Prayer: How Everything Changes When You Seek God's Face* (Grand Rapids, MI: Bethany House Publishers, 2011).

7. How would an understanding of this change the way we pray?

If we were to be honest, our prayers are often motivated by a desire for comfort and convenience. Many times our prayers are viewed as a divinely ordained way to get what we want out of life, or to avoid what we don't want. It is easy to fall into the trap of thinking prayer exists so God can be used to help us preserve our glory rather than our being used to promote His glory. — Daniel Henderson and Jim Cymbala, *Transforming Prayer: How Everything Changes When You Seek God's Face* (Grand Rapids, MI: Bethany House Publishers, 2011).

8. Greear raises an important question about this: Does God have an ego problem?

Think for a moment about God's priority. God exists to showcase God.

Why do the heavens exist? The heavens exist to "declare the glory of God" (Ps. 19:1).

Why did God choose the Israelites? Through Isaiah he summoned "everyone who is called by My name, whom I have created for My glory" (Isa. 43:7 NKJV).

Why do people struggle? God answers, "I have tested you in the furnace of affliction. For My own sake, for My own sake, I will act" (Isa. 48:10–11 NASB). "Call on me when you are in trouble, and I will rescue you, and you will give me glory" (Ps. 50:15 NLT).

God has one goal: God. To proclaim his glory.

God has no ego problem. He does not reveal his glory for his good. We need to witness it for our good.

He responds to our prayers with this goal in mind. If he says no to our requests, it is because his glory matters more than our preferences. — Max Lucado, *Max on Life: Answers and Insights to Your Most Important Questions* (Nashville: Thomas Nelson, 2011).

9. "God's commitment to his glory is good news for us." How so?

Those Divine demands which sound to our natural ears most like those of a despot and least like those of a lover, in fact marshal us where we should want to go if we knew what we wanted. He demands our worship, our obedience, our prostration. Do we suppose that they can do Him any good, or fear, like the chorus in Milton, that human irreverence can bring about 'His glory's diminution'? A man can no more diminish God's glory by refusing to worship Him than a lunatic can put out the sun by scribbling the word 'darkness' on the walls of his cell. But God wills our good, and our good is to love Him (with that responsive love proper to creatures) and to love Him we must know Him: and if we know Him, we shall in fact fall on our faces. — C. S. Lewis, *A Year with C. S. Lewis: Daily Readings from His Classic Works*, ed. Patricia S. Klein, 1st ed. (New York: HarperOne, 2003), 221.

10. How is life better for the person who lives for God's glory? Be specific.

Third, hallowing God's name is for our good. God's glory and Gods love are not at odds. God's desire to be glorified is not opposed to His desire for our joy. Parents want their kids to put their hopes in something solid. We don't want them to think happiness comes ultimately from playing football or going to Yale or getting hammered every weekend. We want their desires to terminate on something that will satisfy. God has the same desire for His children. He wants us to have lasting joy, which is why He directs our attention to His glory. As John Piper says, God is most glorified in us when we are most satisfied in Him. Or to put it another way, our greatest good is to rejoice in God's great glory.

When we pray "Our Father in heaven, hallowed be Your name," we are not only asking for God's fame to spread, among the nations and in our hearts, we are also asking implicitly for our lasting joy. "Not to us, O Lord, not to us, but your name give glory" (Ps. 115:1) is the prayer of a wise and happy man. — Kevin L. DeYoung and Jerry Bridges, *The Good News We Almost Forgot: Rediscovering the Gospel in a 16th Century Catechism* (Chicago, IL: Moody Publishers, 2010).

11. Piper calls it "Christian Hedonism." What does he mean by that?

So I could not agree more with the person who says, "God created us and saves us for His glory!"

"Well, then," my friend asks, "how can you say that the aim of life is to maximize our joy? Didn't God create us to share His ultimate aim—to glorify Himself? Which is it? Are we created for His glory or for our joy?"

Here we are at the heart of Christian Hedonism! If you get anything, get this. I learned it from Jonathan Edwards, C. S. Lewis, and, most importantly, from the apostle Paul.

Edwards was the greatest pastor-theologian that America has ever produced. He wrote a book in 1755 called The End for Which God Created the World. The foundation and aim of that book is the following stunning insight. It is the deepest basis of Christian

Hedonism. Read this old-fashioned English slowly to see Edwards's brilliant resolution.

> God is glorified not only by His glory's being seen, but by its being rejoiced in. When those that see it delight in it, God is more glorified than if they only see it. His glory is then received by the whole soul, both by the understanding and by the heart. God made the world that He might communicate, and the creature receive, His glory; and that it might [be] received both by the mind and heart. He that testifies his idea of God's glory [doesn't] glorify God so much as he that testifies also his ... delight in it.

This is the solution. Did God create you for His glory or for your joy? Answer: He created you so that you might spend eternity glorifying Him by enjoying Him forever. In other words, you do not have to choose between glorifying God and enjoying God. Indeed you dare not choose. If you forsake one, you lose the other. Edwards is absolutely right: "God is glorified not only by His glory's being seen, but by its being rejoiced in." If we do not rejoice in God, we do not glorify God as we ought. — John Piper, *The Dangerous Duty of Delight* (Sisters, OR: Multnomah Publishers, 2001), 18–20.

12. Piper said we glorify God by enjoying Him. We glorify God through our joy. Grumpy people cannot glorify God. Do you agree? How so?

The radical implication is that pursuing pleasure in God is our highest calling. It is essential to all virtue and all reverence. Whether you think of your life vertically in relation to God or horizontally in relation to man, the pursuit of pleasure in God is crucial, not optional. We will see shortly that genuine love for people and genuine worship toward God hang on the pursuit of joy.

Before I saw these things in the Bible, C. S. Lewis snagged me when I wasn't looking. I was standing in Vroman's Bookstore on Colorado Avenue in Pasadena, California, in the fall of 1968. I picked up a thin blue copy of Lewis's book The Weight of Glory. The first page changed my life.

> If there lurks in most modern minds the notion that to desire our own good and earnestly to hope for the enjoyment of it is a bad thing, I submit that this notion has crept in from Kant and the Stoics and is no part of the Christian faith. Indeed, if we consider the unblushing promises of reward and the staggering nature of the rewards promised in the Gospels, it would seem that our Lord finds our desires not too strong, but too weak. We are half-hearted creatures, fooling about with drink and sex and ambition when infinite joy is offered us, like an ignorant child who wants to go on making mud pies in a slum because he cannot imagine what is meant by the offer of a holiday at the sea. We are far too easily pleased.

Never in my life had I heard anyone say that the problem with the world was not the intensity of our pursuit of happiness, but the weakness of it. Everything in me shouted, Yes! That's it! There it was in black and white, and to my mind it was totally compelling: The great problem with human beings is that we are far too easily pleased. We don't seek pleasure with nearly the resolve and passion that we should. And so we settle for mud pies of appetite instead of infinite delight.

Lewis said, "We are far too easily pleased." Almost all of Christ's commands are motivated by "the unblushing promises of reward." Based on "the staggering nature of the rewards promised in the Gospels, it would seem that

our Lord finds our desires not too strong, but too weak."
— John Piper, *The Dangerous Duty of Delight* (Sisters,
OR: Multnomah Publishers, 2001), 21–23.

13. Piper says that pursuing joy in God and praising God are one and the same. You say?

Yes. But what does that have to do with the praise and glory of God? Christian Hedonism says that not only must we pursue the joy that Jesus promises, but also that God Himself is glorified in this pursuit. Lewis helped me see this too.

There was another explosive page, this time from his book Reflections on the Psalms. Here he showed that the very nature of praise is the consummation of joy in what we admire.

> The most obvious fact about praise—whether of God or anything—strangely escaped me.... I had never noticed that all enjoyment spontaneously overflows into praise ... lovers praising their mistresses, readers their favorite poet, walkers praising the countryside.... My whole, more general, difficulty about the praise of God depended on my absurdly denying to us, as regards the supremely Valuable, what we delight to do, what indeed we cannot help doing, about everything else we value. I think we delight to praise what we enjoy because the praise not merely expresses but completes the enjoyment.

So Lewis helped me put it all together. Pursuing joy in God and praising God are not separate acts. "Praise not merely expresses but completes the enjoyment." Worship is not added to joy, and joy is not the by-product of worship. Worship is the valuing of God. And when this valuing is intense, it is joy in God. Therefore the essence of worship is delight in God, which displays His all-satisfying value. — John Piper, *The Dangerous Duty of Delight* (Sisters, OR: Multnomah Publishers, 2001), 23–24.

14. So, is obedience about feeling right, not just believing right and behaving right? Is that right?

Perhaps you can see why it is astonishing to me that so many people try to define true Christianity in terms of decisions and not affections. Not that decisions are unessential. The problem is that they require so little transformation. Mere decisions are no sure evidence of a true work of grace in the heart. People can make "decisions" about the truth of God while their hearts are far from Him.

We have moved far away from the biblical Christianity of Jonathan Edwards. He pointed to 1 Peter 1:8 and argued that "true religion, in great part, consists in the affections."

> Though you have not seen Him, you love Him, and though you do not see Him now, but believe in Him, you greatly rejoice with joy inexpressible and full of glory. (1 Peter 1:8)

Throughout Scripture we are commanded to feel, not just to think or decide. We are commanded to experience dozens of emotions, not just to perform acts of willpower.

For example, God commands us not to covet (Exodus 20:17), and it is obvious that every commandment not to have a certain feeling is also a commandment to have a certain feeling. The opposite of covetousness is contentment, and this is exactly what we are commanded to experience in Hebrews 13:5: "Be content with what you have" (RSV).

God commands us to bear no grudge (Leviticus 19:18). The positive side of not bearing a grudge is forgiving "from the heart." This is what Jesus commands us to do in Matthew 18:35: "Forgive [your] brother from your heart." The Bible does not say, Make a mere decision to drop the grievance. It says, Experience a change in the heart. The Bible goes even further and commands a certain intensity. For example, 1 Peter 1:22 commands "Love one another earnestly from the heart" (RSV). And Romans 12:10 commands "Love one another with brotherly affection" (RSV).

People are often troubled by the teaching of Christian Hedonism that emotions are part of our duty—that they are commanded. This seems strange partly because emotions are not under our immediate control like acts of willpower seem to be. But Christian Hedonism says, "Consider the Scriptures." Emotions are commanded throughout the Bible.

The Scriptures command joy, hope, fear, peace, grief, desire, tenderheartedness, brokenness and contrition, gratitude, lowliness, etc. Therefore Christian Hedonism is not making too much of emotion when it says that being satisfied in God is our calling and duty.

It is true that our hearts are often sluggish. We do not feel the depth or intensity of affections that are appropriate for God or His cause. It is true that at those times we must exert our wills and make decisions that we hope will rekindle our joy. Even though joyless love is not our aim ("God loves a cheerful giver!" 2 Corinthians 9:7; "[Show] mercy with cheerfulness," Romans 12:8), nevertheless it is better to do a joyless duty than not to do it, provided that there is a spirit of repentance that we have not done all of our duty because of the sluggishness of our hearts.

I am often asked what a Christian should do if the cheerfulness of obedience is not there. It's a good question. My answer is not to simply get on with your duty because feelings don't matter. They do! My answer has three steps. First, confess the sin of joylessness. ("My heart is faint; lead me to the rock that is higher than I," Psalm 61:2.) Acknowledge the coldness of your heart. Don't say that it doesn't matter how you feel. Second, pray earnestly that God would restore the joy of obedience. ("I delight to do Your will, O my God; Your Law is within my heart," Psalm 40:8.) Third, go ahead and do the outward dimension of your duty in the hope that the doing will rekindle the delight.

This is very different from saying: "Do your duty because feelings don't count." These steps assume that there is such a thing as hypocrisy. They are based on the belief that our goal is the reunion of pleasure and duty and that a justification of their separation is a justification of sin. — John Piper, *The Dangerous Duty of Delight* (Sisters, OR: Multnomah Publishers, 2001), 28–31.

15. "You cannot place the sun of God's glory into orbit in your life." (Greear) Why not?

Christ Wants to Have First Place in Your Life.

This statement sounds true at first glance, but closer examination will show that it can actually set you on a wrong course in your grace walk. Christ doesn't want to be first place in your life. He wants you to recognize Him as all of your life.

If Jesus Christ wants the first-place spot, what comes second? What about third place? What comes after that? The whole concept is absurd because it implies that our lives can be divided into compartments, with Jesus being one of those compartments.

To understand this point, think about your physical life for a moment. What would you think if I were to suggest that breathing should have first place in your life? What if somebody else said that having a heartbeat should be number one in your life? Maybe someone else could argue, "No, your circulatory system should come first, then breathing, then having a heartbeat."

It's a ridiculous discussion because your body is a whole, unified entity. You can't prioritize which is most important. Your physical health will give expression to every one of those actions in your body. They all work together as they express your normal state of health.

In the same way, our lives are indivisible when it comes to the effect of Christ's presence within us. We can't divide our lives into marriage, parenting, career, hobbies, and so on. All of those areas make up our lifestyle as one unified life, and Jesus is the source of our attitudes and actions in each of those areas. — Steve McVey, *52 Lies Heard in Church Every Sunday: ...and Why the Truth Is so Much Better* (Eugene, OR: Harvest House Publishers, 2011).

16. What does it mean, practically speaking, to put God first in your life?

Many [people] say they cherish the time they spend in prayer during the quiet hours of the early morning. In a truly physical way, they're giving God first place in their day.

Getting up before dawn may not work for you, but putting God first in your thoughts, words, and actions yields extraordinary rewards. You move with God-given purpose, and you gain peace of mind knowing you're doing the right thing for the right reasons. Among the options available to you, choose those things poised to enrich your life and the lives of those around you.

All times of day (or night), let God come first in your life.

Seek those things which are above, where Christ is, sitting at the right hand of God.   Colossians 3:1 NKJV — Baker Publishing Group and Inc. Grq, *365 Moments of Peace for a Woman's Heart: Reflections on God's Gifts of Love, Hope, and Comfort* (Grand Rapids, MI: Bethany House Publishers, 2014).

17. Colossians 3.4. "Christ, who is your life…" What exactly does that mean?

Jesus Christ isn't first place in your life. He is your life. He is the essence of who you are. Paul wrote in Colossians 3:4, "When Christ, who is our life, is revealed, then you also will be revealed with Him in glory." He described life in Philippians 1:21 by saying, "To me, to live is Christ and to die is gain."

Note that Paul didn't give Jesus a high place in his life. Paul realized that the very core of his existence was his union with Jesus Christ. He said it this way in Galatians 2:20: "I have been crucified with Christ; and it is no longer I who live, but Christ lives in me; and the life which I now live in the flesh I live by faith in the Son of God, who loved me and gave Himself up for me."

There it is. Paul said that he didn't have a life apart from Jesus Christ. That's true for you too. While it may sound admirable to say that we want Him to be number one in our lives, it misses the point of our union with Him altogether.

Christ wants to be recognized as the life of your family, career, hobbies, finances, and so on. Do you see the point? He is your everything! — Steve McVey, *52 Lies Heard in Church Every Sunday: ...and Why the Truth Is so Much Better* (Eugene, OR: Harvest House Publishers, 2011).

18. Christ the center. How is the circumference different? How does Christ the center affect our marriage, our work, our parenting?

We do ourselves a disservice when we think that Jesus is a part of our lives, even if it is the number one part. He is the substance of everything that you are. He is our very essence.

You know you're on the right track in your thoughts when you find yourself seeing your marriage relationship as Christ living His life through you, expressing His love and life to your mate. Parenting becomes an expression of His life when we know that He is loving and guiding our children through us. You have a right understanding of priorities when you know He animates your activity at work.

When we know the truth, we stop thinking of Jesus holding first place in our lives and we begin thinking of Jesus being the source that animates every place in our lives. His isn't number one. He's the whole list! — Steve McVey, *52 Lies Heard in Church Every Sunday: ...and Why the Truth Is so Much Better* (Eugene, OR: Harvest House Publishers, 2011).

19. What did you learn today? What do you want to remember?

20. How can we pray for each other this week?

Not God Enough, Lesson #9
Chapter #14: He Wasn't Late After All
Chapter #15: Burning Hearts, Flaming Tongues
Good Questions Have Groups Talking
www.joshhunt.com

OPEN:

Opening question: what is the last funeral you attended.

DIG

1. **John 11. Look over this story. Who can summarize it?**

   When Jesus learns of Lazarus's serious illness, he makes the surprising decision to remain where he is instead of rushing to his friend's bedside. As the story proceeds, the reason for the delay becomes clear: Jesus is waiting for Lazarus to die so that he can raise him up and thereby glorify God.

   By the time Jesus arrives, Lazarus has been dead and buried for four days. Mary and Martha are mourning in the company of "many of the Jews" (11:19). Each sister reproaches Jesus for not coming sooner. Jesus promises Martha that Lazarus will rise again, and declares famously, "I am the resurrection and the life. Those who believe in me, even though they die, will live, and everyone who lives and believes in me will never die" (11:25–26). Martha responds with a full confession of faith: "Yes, Lord, I believe that you are the Messiah, the Son of God, the one coming into the world" (11:27).

Upon seeing Mary, Jesus "was greatly disturbed in spirit, and deeply moved" (11:33). When he sees the tomb, he weeps (11:35). In the first century, Jews were buried in linen shrouds and their bodies laid in a sealed tomb so that the flesh would decompose. After a period of eleven months, the tomb would be unsealed, and the bones would be placed in an ossuary (bone box) and stored on a shelf in the tomb (Hachlili). In the days after burial, however, removing the stone would release the stench of decomposition. Jesus gives thanks to God and clarifies that his prayer is "for the sake of the crowd standing here, so that they may believe that you sent me" (11:41). In doing so, he attributes the miracle not to his own innate power but to God. He then calls out—like the shepherd would to the sheep in John 10—"Lazarus, come out!" thereby fulfilling the prophecy in 5:28–29, that the dead will hear the voice of the Son of God and come out of their tombs (11:43). Lazarus's revival foreshadows Jesus' own. — Raymond Pickett et al., "Jesus and the Christian Gospels," in *The New Testament*, ed. Margaret Aymer, Cynthia Briggs Kittredge, and David A. Sánchez, *Fortress Commentary on the Bible* (Minneapolis, MN: Fortress Press, 2014), 288.

2. What is shocking about Jesus' behavior in this story?

The first astonishing thing in this text is that Jesus did not depart right away so as to get there in time to heal Lazarus. "He stayed two days longer in the place where he was" (v. 6). In other words, he intentionally delayed and let Lazarus die. The second astonishing thing here is that this delay is described as the result of Jesus' love for his friends. Notice the word "so" at the beginning of verse 6: "Jesus loved Martha and her sister and Lazarus. So ... he stayed two days longer." Jesus let Lazarus die because he loved him and his sisters.

What makes sense of this? Jesus gave the answer in verse 4 when he told his disciples why Lazarus was sick: "This illness does not lead to death. It is for the glory of God, so that the Son of God may be glorified through it." Jesus had a plan. He would let Lazarus die so that he could raise him from the dead. This was a costly plan. Lazarus would have to go through the torments of death, and his family would endure four days of grieving over his death. — John Piper, *God Is the Gospel: Meditations on God's Love as the Gift of Himself* (Wheaton, IL: Crossway Books, 2005), 152–153.

3. Verse 6. Why the delay?

But Jesus considers the cost worth it. His explanation has two parts. First, in letting Lazarus die in order to raise him from the dead his aim is to show the glory of God the Father and God the Son. Second, in this costly revelation of his glory he would be loving this family. From this I conclude that the primary way that Jesus loved this family was by doing what he must do to display to them in a compelling way his own glory. — John Piper, *God Is the Gospel: Meditations on God's Love as the Gift of Himself*.(Wheaton, IL: Crossway Books, 2005), 153.

4. Does it appear that Jesus is acting in a loving way?

Many today would call Jesus callous and unloving for letting Lazarus die. And they would add this criticism:

that he is vain and self-conceited if he was motivated by a desire to display his own glory. What this shows is how far above the glory of God most people value pain-free lives. For most people, love is whatever puts human value and human well-being at the highest point. So to call Jesus' behavior loving is unintelligible to them.

But let us learn from Jesus what love is and what our true well-being is. Love is doing whatever you need to do to help people see and savor the glory of God in Christ forever and ever. Love keeps God central. Imitating Jesus in this does not mean that we love by seeking to display our glory. Imitation means that we seek to display his glory. Jesus sought the glory of himself and his Father. We should seek the glory of Jesus and his Father. Jesus is the one being in the universe for whom self-exaltation is the highest virtue and the most loving act. He is God. Therefore the best gift he can give is the revelation of himself. We are not God. Therefore it is not loving for us to point people to ourselves as the ground of their joy. That would be an unloving distraction. Love means helping people see and savor Christ forever. — John Piper, *God Is the Gospel: Meditations on God's Love as the Gift of Himself* (Wheaton, IL: Crossway Books, 2005), 153–154.

5. **What do we learn about God's love for us in this story?**

Mary and Martha sent word to Jesus, about twenty miles away in Bethabara, that the one He loved was sick. I like that! They didn't say, "The one that loves You is sick," but rather, "The one You love is sick." Like Martha and Mary, I don't approach the Lord on the basis of my love for Him. You know why? Because my love for the Lord is fickle and feeble. But His love for me, however, is fixed and firm. He's never surprised by what I say, never taken aback by what I do. Therefore, wise is the man or woman who approaches the Lord based on His love.

Interestingly, the Greek word translated "lovest" is not agapao—the perfect love that gives simply for the sake of giving—but phileo, which refers to affection or friendship. Maybe you think the Lord loves you because He is love and, therefore, has to love you. Not true. Jesus said, "I have not called you servants but friends" (see John 15:15). He doesn't love you simply because He's stuck with you. No, He chose to love you (John 15:16). He loves you as you would love a friend.

Notice that Mary and Martha didn't instruct the Lord concerning what He should do. Oh, how often I make that mistake. I become aware of some problem or need and immediately start instructing the Lord about how He can solve the situation. "Who hath given the Lord counsel?" asked the prophet rhetorically. (Isaiah 40:13). A lot of us try. We would be far wiser to follow the example of Martha and Mary. "Lord, the one who You have affection for is sick," they said. They weren't commanding. They were communing. — Jon Courson, *Jon Courson's Application Commentary* (Nashville, TN: Thomas Nelson, 2003), 531–532.

6. Verses 9, 10. What does daylight represent in these verses?

"Don't worry," answered Jesus. "It's still daylight. There are still things for me to do before the night falls." Oh, night would come soon enough when He would be crucified on a Cross, when His work on earth would cease. But not yet. Consequently, Jesus was implying that He was indestructible. So are you. The Bible says man is appointed unto death (Hebrews 9:27). No matter how many airbags you have in your car, no matter how many injections of vitamin C you take, once your appointed hour comes, that's it. But until that time, you're basically indestructible. Does that mean you can skydive without a parachute? No, for the moment you do will then become your appointed hour. When Satan told Jesus to jump off the temple in order to prove who He was, Jesus said, "It is written thou shalt not tempt the Lord thy God" (see Matthew 4:7). Don't be foolish—but realize there is a period of time in which you can work without being destroyed. — Jon Courson, *Jon Courson's Application Commentary* (Nashville, TN: Thomas Nelson, 2003), 532.

7. Verse 16. Thomas does not get a lot of respect. What do you admire about him from this verse?

I've always liked Thomas. I think he gets a bad rap. He should be remembered not only as the doubting one, but also as the devoted one because watch what he says....

> John 11:16 (b) ...unto his fellow disciples, Let us also go, that we may die with him.

When the other disciples were saying, "Don't go near Jerusalem," Thomas said, "Let's go and die too." I think this shows real devotion and true courage. When Jesus appeared to the disciples in the Upper Room after His Resurrection, Thomas wasn't there (John 20:24). Why? I suggest that while the other guys were hiding in the Upper Room, Thomas was the only one who had the guts to be out on the streets. A lot of times, I think we read things into the lives of Bible characters that aren't totally fair. I think Thomas, for example, is one who deserves a little more credit. — Jon Courson, *Jon Courson's Application Commentary* (Nashville, TN: Thomas Nelson, 2003), 533.

8. How would you evaluate Martha's faith in verse 27?

There's not a believer in this room tonight who doubts the Lord's ability to do a miracle. What we struggle with is the same thing with which Martha struggled. That is, we don't question His ability. But we do question His willingness. Like Martha, we say, "I believe You're Someone special, unique, powerful, the Son of God, Messiah. But I can't believe You would be willing to do something for me." — Jon Courson, *Jon Courson's Application Commentary* (Nashville, TN: Thomas Nelson, 2003), 534.

9. From a human perspective, how was Lazarus death and resurrection tied to Jesus' death and resurrection?

John 11, which has Jesus' seventh sign, links the events that happened at the Jewish feasts and the events of Jesus' suffering and death. It is Lazarus' resurrection, followed by Jesus' triumphant entry into Jerusalem (12:12–19), that eventually lead Jesus to death. There are several events that link John 11 with previous chapters: Jesus' staying two days longer in the place where John at first baptized (10:40) even after hearing of Lazarus' illness (11:6), the attempt to stone at Jesus (11:8), the reference to light and life (11:9–10, 25–26) and to the healing of the man born blind (11:37), the authorities' plan to kill Jesus (11:46–53), and their order to arrest him (11:57). — Jey J. Kanagaraj, John, ed. Michael F. Bird and Craig Keener, *vol. 4, New Covenant Commentary Series* (Eugene, OR: Cascade Books, 2013), 114.

Chapter #15: Burning Hearts, Flaming Tongues

10. 2 Corinthians 5.13 – 15. What made Paul tick? What was in his gas tank?

Paul explains the genius of our own passion: "We have concluded this: that one has died for all . . .; and those who live [should] no longer live for themselves but for him who for their sake died and was raised" (2 Cor 5:14 – 15 ESV). Motivation for mission grows out of deep, personal experience with the gospel. When we are amazed at the grace God showed in saving us, going to great lengths to save others seems an insignificant thing. We yearn to see the glory of our saving God spread throughout the earth and others find in Christ what we have found.

The cross of Christ provided Paul with the motive for sacrifice (love of Christ), a measure for his sacrifice (Christ's death on the cross), and a mission in his sacrifice (seeing people reconciled to God; see 2 Cor. 5:14 – 21). Paul wanted to see others reconciled to God as he had been reconciled. — J. D. Greear and Larry Osborne, *Gaining by Losing: Why the Future Belongs to Churches That Send* (Grand Rapids, MI: Zondervan, 2015).

11. 2 Corinthians 5.13. Why did some people think Paul was just plain crazy?

Paul sacrificed so much for the mission people thought he was a madman (2 Cor. 5:13). When is the last time your sacrifices for the mission made someone question your sanity? When the gospel has really gripped your soul, it produces such levels of sacrifice that people simply have to ask you why you live as you do. You seem to them like a freak who has lost his mind (2 Peter 3:15).

This intensity to do comes only from a deep awareness of what God has done for you. As a friend of mine says, "The fire to do comes from being soaked in the fuel of what has been done." The gospel is the helium that fills the heart with passion and propels us to soar in mission.

Everything in the Christian life grows out of the gospel. Thus, the deeper you and your people go in the gospel, the higher you will soar in the mission. — J. D. Greear and Larry Osborne, *Gaining by Losing: Why the Future Belongs to Churches That Send* (Grand Rapids, MI: Zondervan, 2015).

12. "Compels" seems to be the main verb in this passage. What exactly does it mean?

Paul also spoke of this in 2 Corinthians 5:14, "Christ's love compels us." The context suggests that it is Christ's love as demonstrated on the cross that compels us. The Greek word translated compel suggests that we have no other choice. When we think of what Jesus did for us on the cross, we are compelled to lay down our lives for the cause of Jesus.

The old hymn says it best:

> When I survey the wondrous cross
> On which the Prince of glory died
> My richest gain I count but loss
> And pour contempt on all my pride
>
> Were the whole realm of nature mine
> That were a present far too small
> Love so amazing so divine
> Demands my soul, my life, my all.

The cross demands my soul, my life, my all. There are a million ways that you could express that. Explore as many of them as you can in this life. One good way is by dedicating ourselves to microcosms of the church— small groups that are committed to growing. — Josh Hunt, *Make Your Group Grow*, 2010.

13. Imagine you asked Paul, "Do you like your job?" How do you think he might respond?

When someone asked a missionary if he liked his work in Africa, he replied: "Do I like this work? No, my wife and I do not like dirt. We have reasonably refined sensibilities. We do not like crawling into huts through goats' refuse. We do not like association with ignorant, filthy, brutish people. But is a man to do nothing for Christ he does not like? If not, then God pity him. Liking or disliking has nothing to do with it. We have orders to 'go' and we go. Love constrains us" (2 Cor. 5:14). — AMG Bible Illustrations, *Bible Illustrations Series* (Chattanooga: AMG Publishers, 2000).

14. Romans 10.14 – 15. How does this fuel our motivation to spread the gospel?

We must never minimize the missionary outreach of the church. While this passage relates primarily to Israel, it applies to all lost souls. They cannot be saved unless they call upon the Lord Jesus Christ. But they cannot call unless they believe. Faith comes by hearing (v. 17), so they must hear the message. How will they hear? A messenger must go to them with the message. But this means that God must call and send the messenger (vv. 14–15). What a privilege it is to be one of His messengers and have beautiful feet!

Just the other day, a businessman in our church called me to report another soul led to Christ. My caller had

had serious spiritual problems a few years earlier, and I was able to help him. Since that time, he had led many to Christ. His phone call was to give me the good news that one of his work associates had led a friend to Christ, another miracle in a spiritual chain reaction.

Some of us share the news here at home, but others are sent to distant places. There are more open doors for the gospel than ever before. Do you have beautiful feet? — Warren W. Wiersbe, *Pause for Power: A 365-Day Journey through the Scriptures* (Colorado Springs, CO: David C. Cook, 2010).

15. Romans 1.14 – 16. What exactly is the gospel?

The good news of the gospel is that God makes dead hearts alive. God turns hearts of stone into hearts of flesh. He transformed Saul, Jesus-hating murderer, enemy #1 of the early church, into Paul, its greatest spokesman and missionary. He can do that for you, too. You just have to ask Him. — J. D. Greear and Jason Gaston, *Stop Asking Jesus into Your Heart: The Teen Edition* (Nashville, TN: B&H, 2018).

16. Paul uses a word that could means he was in debt. What does he mean that he is in debt?

In Romans 1:14 Paul uses a strange word to encapsulate his life and calling, one with enormous implications for both church leaders and members alike. "I am under obligation," Paul says, to everyone who has not yet heard the gospel (see ESV). Many translations render "under obligation" as "debtor," because Paul is invoking language that describes a debtor's relationship to his creditor.

When you are severely in debt, your life no longer really belongs to you. It belongs to the creditor. You can't spend money however you would like anymore. If your boss gives you a $10,000 Christmas bonus, you won't be able to use it to take a vacation to Hawaii or to buy new furniture. The creditor has first and final say in how the money is spent. I once knew a church that was so severely in debt that representatives from the bank literally stood in the back of the lobby during the weekly offering, taking the money straight to the bank, where bank officials would decide how much the church could keep that week. The church was no longer free; it was "under obligation."

Paul thought of himself as a debtor to those who had not heard about Jesus. His future was not free. But why did he owe them? Because he knew he was no more deserving of the gospel than they were. He was not more righteous, nor had God seen more potential in him (see 1 Timothy 1:15). Paul saw God's grace toward him exactly for what it was — completely unmerited favor. Paul knew that placed him under severe obligation to the grace of God. Paul's future, bright as it may have been, having a great education and all the right connections, no longer belonged to him. Every spare resource — every ounce of energy, every moment of his time — belonged to his "creditor": the grace of God.

Every person who knows and understands the gospel is under this same debt of obligation. As David Platt says, "Every saved person this side of heaven owes the gospel to every unsaved person this side of hell." If you are saved, you are under obligation to leverage your life to bring salvation to the nations. Those of us called to be leaders in the church are under obligation to train you up and send you out. — J. D. Greear and Larry Osborne, *Gaining by Losing: Why the Future Belongs to Churches That Send* (Grand Rapids, MI: Zondervan, 2015).

17. What would it mean for Paul, if he did not share the gospel?

Paul says in Romans 1:14 that for him not to take the Gospel to people who had never heard it would be stealing. Paul said, "God revealed himself to me through no merit or my own ..." how could I withhold it? I am a debtor. — J. D. Greear, "Thou Shalt Be Generous: Exodus 20:15," in *J. D. Greear Sermon Archive* (Durham, NC: The Summit Church, 2017), Ex 20:15.

18. The gospel is the power of God. Power. In what way is the gospel power?

Only one thing in the Bible is called "the power of God." God does many things by his power, but only one thing is itself called "the power of God." That is the gospel.

Ps. 8. God made the universe with his finger. If the Milky Way were the size of North America, our solar system would be a coffee cup. Earth would be a speck of dust inside the cup. And each us is a speck on the speck inside that cup.

God made this with his finger—it didn't even take his arm, just his finger. Yet he never calls that "creation" the power of God. He calls the gospel his power. Mary says in the gospel is the strength of God's ARM. — J. D. Greear, "Blessed: Luke 1:46–56," *in J. D. Greear Sermon Archive* (Durham, NC: The Summit Church, 2017), Lk 1:46–56.

19. What did you learn today? What do you want to remember?

20. How can we pray for each other this week?

Not God Enough, Lesson #10
Chapter #16: Heaven At Your Back
Chapter #17: Bold Faith in a Big God
Good Questions Have Groups Talking
www.joshhunt.com

OPEN:

Opening question: what is one thing you have learned through this study so far?

DIG

1. **Exodus 3 – 4. Take sixty seconds to look over this story silently. Who can summarize this story?**

   You have been created to be a part of God's redemptive mission in the world. You weren't sent to Planet Earth just to eat food and make a living; you were meant to experience and carry out God's dream. Part of identifying that dream is to encounter a burning bush.

   Let's look at how it happened for Moses in Exodus 3. By that time, Moses had been living in the land of Midian for forty years, taking care of his father-in-law's flock. One day he was tending the sheep near Horeb, a place known as the "mountain of God," when he spotted a bush that appeared to be on fire and yet wasn't being burned up. Not surprisingly, that got Moses' attention, so he stopped to check it out.

The Lord spoke to him from within the bush, directing Moses to remove his sandals because he was standing on holy ground. Frightened, Moses hid his face. But God went on: "The cry of the Israelites has now come to me; I have also seen how the Egyptians oppress them. So come, I will send you to Pharaoh to bring my people, the Israelites, out of Egypt" (Exodus 3:9-10 NRSV). — Mike Slaughter, *Dare to Dream Preview Book: Creating a God-Sized Mission Statement for Your Life* (Nashville: Abingdon Press, 2013).

2. There are numerous applications from this passage. What ones do you see?

Imagine you are Moses on that bizarre day long ago. You're out tending to your father-in-law's sheep, minding your own business, when suddenly, you see a bush on fire. You go in for a closer look, and the voice from the bush identifies itself as the voice of God. Then God tells you to take off your sandals.

If God appeared to us in a burning bush, we would naturally show respect to him. But we are also to respect God when he doesn't show up in miraculous ways. In the course of our daily lives, we need to remember that we are still dealing with the same God who can speak from a burning bush. We should still show God the same awe, respect, humility and obedience that Moses showed God that day.

God is more than worthy of our respect. Considering his almighty power and the fact that he's the one who made us, respecting him is really the least we can do. — Christopher D. Hudson, *NIV, Once-a-Day: At the Table Family Devotional, Ebook* (Grand Rapids, MI: Zondervan, 2012).

3. Exodus 3.10. God has great dreams for Moses. How does Moses feel about these dreams?

What a contrast is Isaiah's response to ours! Christian writer and speaker Jill Briscoe wrote a book she humorously titled: Here Am I—Send Aaron. She was referring to Moses' response when God called him to lead His people out of Egypt to the land He had promised them. Unlike Isaiah, Moses made excuses— "Who am I that I should go? . . . What shall I tell them? . . . What if they do not believe me or listen to me and say, 'The LORD did not appear to you'? . . . I have never been eloquent. . . . Please send someone else." Eventually, in anger, God told him to take his brother Aaron to be his mouthpiece (see Exodus 3–4).

Let's not be too hard on Moses. Under the same circumstances, we, too, might have responded, "Here am I, Lord—send Aaron." Moses had fled Egypt forty years earlier because he was wanted on a murder charge. He had no idea what reaction he would get in Egypt. Of course, we know the end of the story—God used Moses in a mighty way.

What is God asking you to do? Perhaps you think it's far beyond your abilities? If He calls you, He will also enable you, as He did with Moses. I hope you will respond, "Here am I, Lord—send me." — Darlene Sala, *You Are Chosen: Inspiration to Reassure Your Soul* (Uhrichsville, OH: Barbour, 2014).

4. Is this typical? Can you think of other stories of people's calling?

In the Bible, when God calls someone to do something, no one responds by saying, "I'm ready":

- Moses: "I have never been eloquent . . . I am slow of speech and tongue." (Exodus 4:10)

- Gideon: "How can I save Israel? My clan is the weakest in Manasseh, and I am the least in my family." (Judges 6:15)

- Abraham: "Will a son be born to a man a hundred years old?" (Genesis 17:17)

- Jeremiah: "Alas, Sovereign LORD, . . . I am too young." (Jeremiah 1:6)

- Isaiah: "Woe to me! . . . For I am a man of unclean lips." (Isaiah 6:5)

- Esther: "For any man or woman who approaches the king . . . without being summoned the king has but one law: . . . death." (Esther 4:11)

- Rich Young Ruler: "He went away sad, because he had great wealth." (Matthew 19:22)

- Ruth: "There was a famine in the land." (Ruth 1:1)

- Saul (Samuel was going to anoint Saul king; they couldn't find him and asked if he was present.): "And the LORD said, 'Yes, he has hidden himself among the supplies.'" (1 Samuel 10:22) — John Ortberg, *What Is God's Will for My Life?* (Carol Stream, IL: Tyndale House Publishers, Inc., 2016).

5. **Genesis 17.17. This is actually the second calling of Abraham. How does he feel about the vision God has for his life?**

Too inarticulate, too weak, too old, too young, too sinful, too dangerous, too rich, too poor, too much baggage —

no one ever says, "Okay, Lord —I feel ready." And God says to us what he has always said: "Ready or not . . ."

Feeling ready is highly overrated. God isn't looking for readiness; he's looking for obedience. When God brought the people of Israel into the Promised Land, he had them step into the Jordan first, then he parted the river. If they had waited for proof, they'd be standing on the banks still.

Pastor Craig Groeschel put God's determination to use us like this: "If you're not dead, you're not done."

Abraham was seventy-five years old when God promised him a son. He had to wait an additional twenty-four years. He made numerous wrong choices. He lied and said that Sarah was his sister rather than his wife (twice!). He slept with Sarah's servant when it seemed like God was never going to act.

When God repeated his promise, "Abraham fell facedown; he laughed and said to himself, 'Will a son be born to a man a hundred years old? Will Sarah bear a child at the age of ninety?'" (Genesis 17:17).

"Sarah will bear you a son," God responded (Genesis 17:19). "I don't care how old she is." If you're not dead, you're not done.

Abraham tries to say no because he's too old. Timothy tries to say no because he's too young. Esther tries to say no because she's the wrong gender. Moses tries to say no because he has the wrong gifts. Gideon tries to say no because he's from the wrong tribe. Elijah tries to say no because he has the wrong enemy. Jonah tries to say no because he's being sent to the wrong city. Paul tries to say no because he has the wrong background. God keeps saying, "Go, go. You go." Sometimes it takes a while for God's promises to be fulfilled. But if you're not dead, that's the clue you're not done. — John Ortberg, *What Is God's Will for My Life?* (Carol Stream, IL: Tyndale House Publishers, Inc., 2016).

6. **Perhaps someone is thinking, "I am too old to do anything great for God." What would you say to them?**

If you're not dead, you're not done. In the Bible, age is never a reason for someone to say no when God says go. Moses is eighty years old when God calls him to go to Pharaoh and lead the children of Israel out of Egypt. The Exodus starts when he's eighty. Caleb is eighty when he asks God to give him one more mountain to take in the Promised Land.

Florence Detlor, a woman at the church where I work, decided a few years ago that she needed a new challenge, so she went on Facebook.

She was 101 years old at the time.

It turns out that out of the one billion or so people who were on Facebook, Florence Detlor was the oldest. In fact, when Mark Zuckerberg found out, he invited Florence Detlor from our church to go to Facebook headquarters on a personal tour and have her picture taken with him and Sheryl Sandberg.

When the first television interview went public, in a single day Florence got seven thousand friend requests. Seven thousand people from around the world said, "Florence, would you be my friend?" She says she's getting carpal tunnel syndrome trying to respond to requests for her friendship —at the age of 101. If you're not dead, you're not done. — John Ortberg, *All the Places to Go . . . How Will You Know? God Has Placed*

before You an Open Door. What Will You Do? (Carol
Stream, IL: Tyndale House Publishers, Inc., 2015).

7. What if God calls and I say no. What bad things will happen?

Some of the saddest stories are about calls that never
get answered, risks that never get taken, obedience that
never gets offered, joyful generosity that never gets
given, adventures that never happen, lives that never
get lived. I hope that's not you.

There is an entire field of study in the social sciences
around the psychology of regret. One of the most
striking findings is the way that regret changes over
the course of our lives. Short-term regrets most often
involve wishing we hadn't done something: I wish I
hadn't eaten that peach cobbler. I wish I hadn't asked
that girl out and been rejected.

The world of social media even has an acronym for this
one: YOLO — "you only live once." This is associated
with the reckless pursuit of fun while throwing off the
consequences of reason and responsibility. It is most
often used when you choose the unfortunate option.
"Who knew the highway patrol was so picky about
texting while doing 85 mph? —YOLO."

But over time, our perspective shifts. As we get older, we
come to regret those actions that we did not take. The
word of love we never spoke. The chance to serve we
never took. The costly gift we never gave.

We begin our lives regretting the wrong things we have
done, but we end them regretting the open doors we
never went through. What do we need to do now so
that we're not living in regret then? Walking through
open doors keeps us from future regrets. We may have

short-term regrets if we make the wrong choice, but going through open doors keeps us from wondering what might have been.

The divine "go" comes into every life, but we must be willing to leave before we're willing to go. — John Ortberg, *All the Places to Go . . . How Will You Know? God Has Placed before You an Open Door. What Will You Do?* (Carol Stream, IL: Tyndale House Publishers, Inc., 2015).

8. **What (almost) kept Moses from following God's call? Was it rebellion against God, or something else?**

Few of us would think of Moses as having low self–esteem. But read his answer when God told him that he would be the one to lead Israel out of bondage: "Who am I, that I should go to Pharaoh, and that I should bring the sons of Israel out of Egypt?" (Ex. 3:11 NASB).

Even after God confirmed His support, Moses continued to struggle: "Please, Lord, I have never been eloquent, neither recently nor in time past, nor since Thou hast spoken ... for I am slow of speech and slow of tongue" (Ex 4:10 NASB).

If you have ever felt this way, you are not alone. However, God has a course mapped out for your life, and all the inadequacies in the world will not change His mind. He will be with you every step of the way. And though it may take time, He has a celebration planned for when you cross over the "Red Seas" of your life.

Moses was right. He had nothing to say on his own. But the moment he trusted the Lord to be his support, things changed—seas parted, pillars of fire rose in the night, and water flowed from rocks.

In God's eyes there are no losers, only lives being changed for His glory. The cure for inferiority is the staff of God's righteousness. Grasp it and move forward to meet the challenge He has placed before you. — Charles F. Stanley, *Enter His Gates: A Daily Devotional* (Nashville: Thomas Nelson Publishers, 1998).

9. Exodus 3.12. What was God's solution to Moses's insecurity? Did God say to Moses, "You are great! You are strong! You can do it! You got to believe!"

God had an assignment for Moses and called to him from a burning bush. Moses had been chosen by God to lead the Israelites out of Egypt to the Promised Land. However, Moses did not immediately embrace God's plan. He came up with excuse after excuse why he couldn't obey.

Moses was hesitant to approach Pharaoh and ask for the Israelites' freedom. The Lord responded to Moses by assuring him that He would be with him. The Lord wanted Moses to depend on Him rather than himself.

The same is true for us today. When the Lord gives us a divine assignment, He will be with us. He will meet our needs and enable us to accomplish His will. God wants us to totally depend on Him. — Julie Rayburn, *Be Still and Know. . .: 365 Devotions for Abundant Living* (Uhrichsville, OH: Barbour Books, 2017).

10. Is this how God normally deals with our insecurity?

"I am holy. I am merciful. I am ever-present." This is what God says to Moses in verse 12. Isn't this what we saw all throughout Genesis? When we were reading the Patriarchs, we saw God saying, "I will be with you," "I will be with you," "I will be with you," over and over and over again. Now, He comes to Moses. Now, let's put ourselves in Moses' bare feet here for a second. You're talking to a bush, and God says to you, a slave, a commoner, a shepherd, a common person, "You're going to go to the ruler of all the land, Pharaoh, and you're going to tell him to let all of his slaves go." Moses immediately starts saying what you and I would probably say, "Why me? What do you mean I'm going to do this?" I love how God responds to this. Notice what God doesn't say. What you don't see God say is, "Well, listen, bro, like, you're the best shot we've got in this deal. You grew up in Pharaoh's court. You know the Egyptians. You know the Hebrews pretty well, too. So, man, we were looking in the minors, and you were the best prospect we have. So, we're going to pull you out, and this is ... you can do this, man." No, thankfully.

Now, some of those things are true about Moses. God had, no question, sovereignly directed every step toward this end. Isn't it good to know there's a God who is working behind the scenes and who's bringing, orchestrating, all of this together for our good and His glory? Certainly, all those things were true, but God doesn't say, "Moses, here's why I chose you. Here's this qualification, this qualification, this qualification." He says, "I will be with you." In other words, "Moses, it doesn't matter who you are, bro, I am with you. This is not about you as much as it is about me."

What if God ... what if God actually chooses to call us to things in our lives, not because of our qualifications and our abilities, but in order to lead us to a place where we are radically dependent on His presence? This is what we see all throughout Scripture, isn't it? All these heroes of the faith in the Old Testament? Joshua 1:5, "Joshua, I will be with you. I will never leave you nor forsake you." We sang about that. Judges 6, "Gideon, I will be with you." Jeremiah 1:8, "Jeremiah, I will be with you." Don't miss it: the call to God's service is always accompanied by the promise of God's presence. The call to God's service is always accompanied by the promise of God's presence.

Mom or dad in this room, feeling overwhelmed? Man or woman in this room, feeling overwhelmed? Work ... the situation that God has put you in? Know this: God is Yahweh, the ever-present one who does not leave His people alone. — David Platt, "Yahweh," in *David Platt Sermon Archive* (Birmingham, AL: David Platt, 2010), 2418–2419.

Chapter #17: Bold Faith in a Big God

11. John Newton wrote,

**Thou art coming to a King,
Large petitions with thee bring;
For his grace and power are such,
None can ever ask too much.**

Is this biblical? Should we come to God with large petitions?

I think our prayers are too timid. We pray for Aunt Susie's ingrown toenail when we need to pray for world revival. We pray to get through this financial hump when we should pray that earth would become a little more like Heaven. God, make us people of big, bold prayers. — Josh Hunt, *The Habit of Discipleship* (Pulpit Press, 2015).

12. James 4.1 – 3. Complete this sentence. "You do not have because…"

There's a little fable about a Mr. Jones who dies and goes to heaven. Peter is waiting at the gates to give him a tour. Amid the splendor of golden streets, beautiful mansions, and choirs of angels that Peter shows him, Mr. Jones notices an odd-looking building. He thinks it looks like an enormous warehouse—it has no windows and only one door. But when he asks to see inside, Peter hesitates. "You really don't want to see what's in there," he tells the new arrival.

Why would there be any secrets in heaven? Jones wonders. What incredible surprise could be waiting for me in there? When the official tour is over he's still wondering, so he asks again to see inside the structure.

Finally Peter relents. When the apostle opens the door, Mr. Jones almost knocks him over in his haste to enter. It turns out that the enormous building is filled with row after row of shelves, floor to ceiling, each stacked neatly with white boxes tied in red ribbons.

"These boxes all have names on them," Mr. Jones muses aloud. Then turning to Peter he asks, "Do I have one?"

Peter follows, shaking his head. He catches up with Mr. Jones just as he is slipping the red ribbon off his box and popping the lid. Looking inside, Jones has a moment of instant recognition, and   "These boxes all have names on them," Mr. Jones muses. Turning to Peter he asks, "Do I have one?"

"Yes, you do." Peter tries to guide Mr. Jones back outside. "Frankly," Peter says, "if I were you...." But Mr. Jones is already dashing toward the "J" aisle to find his box. He lets out a deep sigh like the ones Peter has heard so many times before.

Because there in Mr. Jones's white box are all the blessings that God wanted to give to him while he was on earth...but Mr. Jones had never asked.

"Ask," promised Jesus, "and it will be given to you" (Matthew 7:7). "You do not have because you do not ask," said James (James 4:2). Even though there is no limit to God's goodness, if you didn't ask Him for a blessing yesterday, you didn't get all that you were supposed to have. — Bruce Wilkinson, *Prayer of Jabez*

13. Matthew 13.58. What prevents God from doing miracles?

I wonder how many miracles He has not done among us because of our lack of faith. I wonder how many unanswered prayers. I wonder how many unprayed prayers. I wonder how many unchanged lives. — Josh Hunt, *How to Live the Christian Life*, 2016.

14. Isaiah 40.5. What do we learn about God from this verse?

But now consider how God stands related to those mighty forces which you fear so much. "Surely the nations are like a drop in a bucket, they are regarded as dust on the scales;. . . Before him all the nations are as nothing; they are regarded by him as worthless and less than nothing" (Is 40:15, 17). You tremble before the nations, because you are much weaker than they; but God is so much greater than the nations that they are as nothing to him. Behold your God!

Look next at the world. Consider the size of it, the variety and complexity of it, think of the nearly five thousand millions who populate it, and of the vast sky above it. What puny figures you and I are, by comparison with the whole planet on which we live! Yet what is this entire mighty planet by comparison with God? "He sits enthroned above the circle of the earth, and its people are like grasshoppers. He stretches out the heavens like a canopy, and spreads them out like a tent to live in" (Is 40:22). The world dwarfs us all, but God dwarfs the world. — J.I. Packer, *Knowing God*, 1973.

15. Occasionally I will hear someone pray and say something like, "Lord, if you can…" What is wrong with this picture?

Sometimes we pray like, "Father, I do not know if you can do this or not." But when you intercede for someone, it is like a guided missile. It is instantaneous. And it is on target. Carolyn T. Ritzman, Claude King, and W. Oscar Thompson, *Concentric Circles of Concern: From Self to Others through Life-Style Evangelism* (Nashville: B&H, 1999).

16. 2 Corinthians 12.7 – 9. What do we learn about prayer from this passage?

When you are happy, so happy that you have no sense of needing Him, so happy that you are tempted to feel His claims upon you as an interruption, if you remember yourself and turn to Him with gratitude and praise, you will be—or so it feels—welcomed with open arms. But go to Him when your need is desperate, when all other help is vain, and what do you find? A door slammed in your face, and a sound of bolting and double bolting on the inside. After that, silence. You may as well turn away. The longer you wait, the more emphatic the silence will become. There are no lights in the windows. It might be an empty house. Was it ever inhabited? It seemed so once. And that seeming was as strong as this. What can this mean? Why is He so present a commander in our time of prosperity and so very absent a help in time of trouble? — C. S. Lewis, *A Grief Observed* (HarperOne, 1996)

17. Matthew 6.7. Should we pray long prayers or short prayers?

The point of Jesus' instruction is not that we should necessarily utter short prayers before God (see Matthew 26:44; Luke 6:12; 18:1)—although short prayers are just fine if that is all you have time for or if that meets your particular need at the moment. The point of Jesus' instruction is that we should not engage in endless babbling, repeating the same request over and over again within the confines of a single prayer, as if that would force God's hand to answer. — Ron Rhodes, *5-Minute Apologetics for Today: 365 Quick Answers to Key Questions* (Eugene, OR: Harvest House, 2010).

18. Matt 21:22. Why do you suppose God chose faith as the pipe through which answered prayers flow? Why not righteousness or something else?

Faith must accept the answer given by God in heaven before it is found on earth. This is the essence of believing prayer. Spiritual things can only be spiritually grasped. The spiritual blessing of God's answer to your prayer must be accepted in your spirit before you see it physically. Faith does this.

A person who not only seeks an answer, but first seeks after the God who gives the answer, receives the power to know that he has obtained what he has asked. If he knows that he has asked according to God's will, he believes that he has received.

There is nothing so heart-searching as this faith, "if you believe, you will have it." As we strive to believe, and find we cannot, we are compelled to discover what hinders us. Blessed are those who, with their eyes on God alone, refuse to rest till they have believed what our Lord bids. Here is the place where faith prevails, and prevailing prayer is born out of human weakness. Here enters the real need for persevering prayer that will not rest or go away or give up till it knows it is heard and believes that it has received. — Andrew Murray, *Teach Me to Pray: Lightly-Updated Devotional Readings from the Works of Andrew Murray* (Uhrichsville, OH: Barbour, 2012).

19. What have you learned from this study? How do you want to live differently because of this study?

May we stretch out our hands, stand on our tiptoes, and pray. Let's pray big, audacious, impossible prayers. And may we continue to listen, to learn, and to obey. Anything is possible with God.

Bold prayers honor God, and God honors bold prayers. God isn't offended by your biggest dreams or boldest prayers. He is offended by anything less. If your prayers aren't impossible to you, they are insulting to God. Why? Because they don't require divine intervention. But ask God to part the Red Sea, or make the sun stand still or float an iron axhead, and God is moved to omnipotent action. There is nothing God loves more than keeping promises, answering prayers, performing miracles, and fulfilling dreams. That is who He is. That is what He does. — Susie Larson and John Eldredge, *Your Powerful Prayers: Reaching the Heart of God with a Bold and Humble Faith* (Grand Rapids, MI: Bethany House Publishers, 2016).

20. How can we pray for each other today?